THE ELEMENTARY SCHOOL OF THE FUTURE
A Guide for Parents

THE ELEMENTARY SCHOOL OF THE FUTURE

A Guide for Parents

By

CARL H. DELACATO, Ed.D.

Director, The Developmental Reading Program
Chestnut Hill Academy
Director, The Institute for Language Disability
Director, Psychological Services
The Institutes for the Achievement of Human Potential
Philadelphia, Pennsylvania

CHARLES C THOMAS · PUBLISHER
Springfield · Illinois · U.S.A.

Published and Distributed Throughout the World by
CHARLES C THOMAS • PUBLISHER
BANNERSTONE HOUSE
301-327 East Lawrence Avenue, Springfield, Illinois, U.S.A.
NATCHEZ PLANTATION HOUSE
735 North Atlantic Boulevard, Fort Lauderdale, Florida, U.S.A.

With THOMAS BOOKS careful attention is given to all details of manufacturing and design. It is the Publisher's desire to present books that are satisfactory as to their physical qualities and artistic possibilities and appropriate for their particular use. THOMAS BOOKS will be true to those laws of quality that assure a good name and good will.

N-2
Printed in the United States of America

To the students of Chestnut Hill Academy—who have taught me for the past twenty years.

Preface

Elementary education is in crisis. Elementary education is also in transition. It has been in some critical or transitive state for most of its history. Its critics are impatient. They insist that elementary education take on a more stolid or a more dynamic mantle. In most part, such critics suggest revolutionary changes in one direction or another depending upon their personal bias.

Elementary education is the result of an evolutionary process and so should be its course toward the future and the ideal. The author feels that much of the anxiety relative to elementary education would be dispelled if its critics were aware of the forces which establish trends in education, were cognizant of today's educational practices and the theories behind them, and were able to see the logical and necessary transition of present theories and practices as they will become the theories and practices of the ideal school of the future through the never ceasing mechanics of evolution.

This book is an attempt to point up what the end product or the ideal elementary school of the future will be. The author feels that through an analysis of the areas of transition and evolution one can visualize the end product.

Because of the complexity of a social institution of long standing, such as the elementary school, the author feels that the analysis should be made at a relatively specific level. The author feels that published materials on education for the general public are constantly aimed at philosophic and generalized levels, hence the patrons of our elementary schools are really uninformed about the real meanings of school practices and changes thereof at the day-to-day level. He has, therefore, analyzed the elementary school into its component parts and has indicated the trends which those specific areas of the school will follow in their evolution toward the ideal. Having visualized the ideal toward which the various facets of the elementary school are growing, the author feels that one can be more understanding of and helpful in dealing with the transitional weaknesses and slow changes which will eventuate in the ideal elementary school of the future.

Contents

THE ELEMENTARY SCHOOL OF THE FUTURE
A Guide for Parents

CHAPTER I

The Educational Frontier in Transition

Why Have The Schools Changed?

(The education of the young has been criticized throughout the history of civilization.) The most recent surge of criticism can be roughly traced back to the days of World War I when industry and the military found inadequacies in the product which they received from the schools and colleges. It was felt that there was a dearth of the "inquiring mind" and "the adventuresome spirit" to meet the challenges of a new and constantly changing environment. Many noted that education, prior to the war, was turned toward teaching "culture" through a method which spent much time in emphasizing the disciplinary values of studying the classics. This educational system seemed to have produced many individuals who were unable to deal with the dynamic challenges of a new era. The public wanted its schools to change. Many schools resisted the subsequent public pressure and taught as they had always taught. These schools were soon labeled "conservative." A second group of schools yielded to public pressure and broke away from the conservatives. They espoused the teaching theories of John Dewey and were labeled "progressive." The progressive schools emphasized a type of teaching which was related almost exclusively to children's interests. The progressives made school and learning seem like fun. Children approached learning through "units of interest" in which socialization and self-expression were stressed. Specific subject matter was introduced only when the somewhat capricious interests of children fell upon it.

These conflicting schools of thought existed side by side dur-

ing the period between the two World Wars. Schools allied themselves with one camp or another, some few trying the middle of
the road. A very good analysis of the two conflicting schools of
thought was made by J. S. Brubacher in 1939.[1] Brubacher also
added the name of the educator who was the most successful in
stressing each characteristic of the opposing schools of thought.

PROGRESSIVE EDUCATION

Characteristics		*Educators*
	Freedom	John Dewey
	Independent thinking	Boyd Bode
	Initiative	W. H. Kilpatrick
	Self-reliance	Carleton Washburne
	Interests, urges and needs	Ralph Tyler
	Social orientation	Carson Ryan
Pupil	Social organization and shared experience	Lester Dix
	Problem solving	James Tippet
	Activity	Caroline Zachry
	Individuality	E. L. Thorndike
	Self-expression	Harold Rugg
	Purposeful learning	George Counts
	Connection with normal life outside of school	Murray and Doris Lee
		Alice Keliher
		Harold Hand

Guidance of the child
Development of the "whole" child
Democratic sharing between pupil and teacher
Individual differences
Change and novelty
No final or fixed values in advance
Constant revision of aims
Experimental techniques of learning and teaching
Education as reconstructor of society

TRADATIONAL EDUCATION

Characteristics		*Educators*
	Freedom as social privilege	W. C. Bagley
	Freedom as an outcome, not as a means of education	H. H. Horne
		M. Demiashkevich
	Discipline as needed in life	T. H. Briggs
	Learning as a realization, not a creation	H. C. Morrison
Pupil	Initiative as self-disciplining activity	Franklin Bobbitt
	Interests as a part of law and order in the universe	
	Intellectual development	
	Learning for future use	
	Gap between school life and the outside world	

[1]*Modern Philosophies of Education:* McGraw-Hill Book Company, 1939, Chap. XIV.

Education as eternal striving for the perfect or absolute
Training of the child for adaptation to the mores of society
Certain fixed educational values
Set curriculum
Minimum essentials which all must learn, such as the classics in literature, mathematics, history and science
Education as conformity to the laws of the universe
Education as creature, not creator of society
Education as the process of transmission of the heritage and culture of the race

Parents were gradually becoming aware of the dissimilarity in theory and practice of the two groups at the outbreak of World War II. The War made re-evaluation of education a necessity. The products of both types of schools exhibited weaknesses in certain areas of development. The progressive school produced students who had intellectual curiosity and imagination but who lacked the necessary habit patterns and academic skills to be effective. The conservative schools produced students who were well grounded in the academic areas and in the mechanics of the culture but who lacked the imaginative intellect and adequate freedom of personality to cope with new problems effectively.

Neither system had fully met the needs of our national community.

During the war a new force became evident. It was the force of the mental hygiene movement. This new and dynamic force added another facet to education's conflict. It took the formulation of philosophies of education out of the realm of pure logical analysis by the introduction of a complex redefinition of "childrens needs." It brought to education a body of literature which stressed the education of the "whole child," that is, education which stresses both the academic and the social-emotional growth of the child. This new factor threw the conflicting schools of thought into an even more noticeable imbalance.

The elementary school is now making an adjustment to the three forces. The mental hygiene movement has acted as a catalyst in its evolution and is speeding the process. It is also providing many avenues for the "coming together" of both schools of thought.

The school of the future must fuse the best aspects of these three forces. It must use those aspects of the culture which are of true value and must discard those aspects which do not make a contribution toward a fuller life for the individual. The elementary school of the future must provide healthy habits of self-expression without the tendency toward unlimited or promiscuous self-expression. It must do all of these things within the framework of providing for good mental health on the part of each child.

Because of the instability of the post war world and because the "democratic versus communistic" conflict is heightened, there is also involved the element of urgency. Public opinion demands that the schools become a true bulwark for democracy. The urgency of the situation demands that the schools overcome their philosophic obstacles and begin to function at such a level wherein the children of the community will be best educated to meet the needs of a somewhat unstable and very challenging atomic age. Many schools have accepted these challenges and are now in the process of becoming the schools on the frontier of the movement toward the realization of the ideal in elementary education.

CHAPTER II

Objectives

What do We Want for Our Children?

Many lists of educational objectives have been published. They are very similar. They differ primarily in the specificity in which they are presented. Educational objectives are in essence a positive representation of the universal needs of children who are to succeed in our culture.

The author, as chairman of the philosophy committee of Chestnut Hill Academy, compiled the following list of objectives from a study of the most universally accepted lists of educational objectives published to date and from an analysis of the needs of individuals in our culture.[1]

Each child must be helped to reach the following objectives in so far as he is able:

1. To be adaptable to change.
2. To develop aesthetic appreciation.
3. To conserve and reclaim human and natural resources.
4. To appreciate the cultural heritage.
5. To practice the basic tenets of democratic living.
6. To develop effective study habits and skills.
7. To grow intellectually.
8. To be mentally healthy.
9. To live in accord with moral and ethical values.

---

[1]The author wishes to acknowledge his indebtedness to Daniel Charles, Christopher Donner and David Heimbach of the faculty of Chestnut Hill Academy for their help in compiling these objectives.

10. To be physically healthy.
11. To develop responsible home membership.
12. To be a responsible and productive member of society.
13. To be healthfully self-expressive.
14. To achieve self-realization.
15. To develop a scientific attitude.
16. To understand spiritual and religious values.
17. To think as a free man.
18. To practice worthy use of leisure time.

The objectives listed above have not been put in any order of importance. They represent the factors which the twentieth century culture requires of each well-adjusted and well-educated individual. The objectives listed above are, of necessity, ideals. We can expect each individual to attain them only in so far as he is able.

The elementary school operates within the overall framework of these cultural objectives. It must, therefore, meet these objectives in the same relationship as its purposes and function dictate. There is abroad, however, at the present time a feeling against the broad elementary school philosophy. There is no doubt that the elementary school of the future will be based on these broad objectives. There will be times wherein certain groups of parents and/or educators attempt to restrict the curriculum to a completely academic basis. These groups make themselves heard periodically on the subject of; "Let's have the elementary school deal with the intellectual aspect of growth; other appropriate agencies such as the home, church, civic organizations and parent groups can deal with such aspects of growth as social development, health and emotional growth." Such forces operating toward the restriction of the program of the elementary school are healthy. They tend to make the elementary school re-evaluate its function in the culture and in so doing, tend to help it maintain a dynamic balance of emphasis within the cultural objectives as accepted in modern America.

Now let us analyze these objectives and attempt to relate them to the latter years of the twentieth century.

To Be Adaptable to Change

The atomic age is a dynamic age. It is an age of constant motion from balance to imbalance to balance. Technological advances are being expressed daily in variations of our mores and values. It has been said of this age that the only stability which exists is the ability to adapt to various ways of dealing with an unstable world.

We want our children to be able to deal with these dynamics and to live happily while doing so. We want them to take change and progress as inevitable growths toward a richer civilization. We want them to deal with these changes in a manner which will enrich their lives and help them to grow with a constantly changing and growing world.

To Develop Aesthetic Appreciation

We want our children to appreciate the beautiful. We want them to be cognizant of the beauties of nature and of those created by man. We want them to relate these beauties, which are in reality deep spiritual experiences, to their daily lives. We want to foster, through the appreciation of beauty, a citizenry which will see that more beauty is put on the earth. We want our children to live in a world where beauty exists, is protected, and is created constantly.

To Conserve and Reclaim Human and Natural Resources

We are coming into an era wherein our natural resources assume a greater importance. With each passing decade we see a greater need to conserve both our human and natural resources. If we are to survive as a nation, we must be cognizant of our future needs and must plan to meet them. Education must constantly lead the way in the solution of this major problem of survival.

Human resources must be conserved if we are to be an effective and productive nation. We have long overlooked a great segment of our population in recruiting helping hands. These are the members of society who do not meet the requirements of the producing mechanism. This group can be reclaimed and added to our national pool of production.

Our natural resources must be conserved. They must be used judiciously. If they have been exploited injudiciously they must be reclaimed. The children of our nation will have to solve these problems in the very near future.

To Appreciate the Cultural Heritage

We want our children to know what has come before them. We want them to profit from the experiences of the past and we want them to use that experience to establish a perspective which will help them to meet the problems of today. We want them to use whatever they choose from the past, not because of any obligation to do so, but to use it because it will be helpful to them to understand the contributions and the mistakes of the past.

To Practice the Basic Tenets of Democratic Living

We want our children to understand and to practice the principles of democracy. We want them to learn to live happily in a world of freedom. We want them to protect this freedom.

If children are expected to live in, appreciate, and protect the democratic way of life, the school and the home must provide a democratic atmosphere in which they can grow. The school must be a democratic organization in which the rights and privileges of the individual are important. Too often in the past the school taught democracy but in practice was an autocratic institution. Democracy begins in the home and is extended through democratic classrooms and through democratically organized schools. Children need these democratic experiences if they are to live democratically as adults.

To Grow Intellectually

There has been a gradual tendency since the beginning of the twentieth century for education in America to change academic standards. Many of these standards have improved with change, but the general inadequacy of the changes rests with the premise that schools have slighted the academic facet of their work. This criticism is valid in many instances. The school of the future must teach children to read, write, and do arithmetic to the best of their ability. It must stress the formation of good academic habits and must maintain standards set by the capacity indications of each child, for each child. Intellectual growth is one of the prime objectives of any educational activity.

Life is rapidly becoming more complex. Each decade requires more academic mastery from the common man. To meet this ever increasing need the school must see that each child achieves academically to the best of his ability.

To Be Mentally Healthy

We want our children to be well-balanced personalities. We want them to take the successes and failures of life in their stride and to be able to deal with them effectively.

We want our children to be sufficiently emotionally mature to be able to deal with the complexities of modern civilization with understanding and with vigor.

Above all, we must as a nation stop the great increase in the numbers of people who are mentally or emotionally unfit to meet fully their obligations to society or who are hospitalized because of mental illness. Not only must this program be preventive, it must also strive to undo the damage of the past and constantly strive toward the rehabilitation of those who have not achieved adequate mental health.

To Be Physically Healthy

Both World Wars have provided evidence pointing up the fact that we are not as healthy a nation as is indicated by our constantly increasing longevity. Too many of our people have physical anomalies which can and should be corrected because they interfere with efficiency in living.

Because of public pressure and because of better facilities and techniques, the medical profession is gradually meeting more of the nation's health needs. In addition to this improvement the schools must educate toward prevention of many of the physical anomalies which now exist. The school of the future must give information and understanding of the factors making for good physical health to each child. It must provide healthful activities for the children during the school year and must provide for the continuity of those activities during the summer and upon graduation from school. Our children must have proper attitudes toward health habits and the care of the body.

To Develop Responsible Home Membership

A major crisis which America faces is the tendency of its homes toward instability. This problem not only deals with the tremendous increase in broken homes, but is also involved with the inability of members of homes, both children and adult, to take their proper position and to assume their proper responsibilities in the home.

We want our children to be responsible and contributing members of their homes. We want them to grow into adults who will have the type of attitudes and habits which will make them worthy home members. We want them to become parents whose feeling for the home and for each person's position in the home will make for happiness for all members of the home. We want our children to become adults who will make the American home the stable institution it must be if we are to continue to grow and be strong as a nation.

To Live in Accord with Moral and Ethical Values

Too often schools have been reluctant to teach moral and ethical values to our children. This has been in part the result of a reticence to justify what education considers moral and ethical standards to be. It is also a result of the tendency of the school and the public to consider the moral and ethical aspects of growth the sole jurisdiction of the home and the church.

Since the beginning of our atomic age our national community has been disturbed about the lack of teaching in the area of morals and ethics on the part of the schools. The feeling is that education has created a scientific monster which could eventuate in complete world destruction or that it has conceived a science which could benefit the world immeasurably, without teaching the moral and ethical concepts which govern the use of these ever advancing scientific discoveries. The school of the future will be required by society not only to teach moral and ethical values to its children, but will be held accountable by the nation if it is not successful in this field.

To Be Responsible and Productive Members of Society

A democracy's strength rests with the individual in the final analysis. If the democratic unit is to be stable each individual must be a responsible member who is willing to assume his proper role in its protection and growth. We want citizens who think and act positively and constructively relative to society as it is and as they hope it will be under ideal conditions.

We want productive citizens who can contribute to the material growth of the group. We want citizens who are self-sufficient and who can through their productivity enrich their lives and those of their fellow citizens. We want a citizenry which, as a group, is productive in all areas. Such a citizenry will further the cause of democracy and make a real contribution to the advancement of our civilization.

To Achieve Self-realization

We want our children to live the fullest lives possible. The basic restriction to this fullness and success should be the limitations of the child himself. We want each child to grow in every way possible, exploiting every capability which contributes to his well being and to the well being of the community. We want to eliminate as soon as possible the arbitrary restrictions set upon opportunity by the culture at the moment and to give every opportunity possible for growth to each child according to his capacity to profit from them.

To Develop a Scientific Attitude

We live in a complex scientific age. Our children will live as adults in an even more complex and scientific age. We want them to be objective about their world. We want them to observe their world lucidly and then through logical analysis and evaluation to reach valid and reliable conclusions.

We want our children to have questioning intellects which will help them to analyze their problems logically and to make judgments which are in keeping with the reality of the data at hand. We want them to be keen observers of their universe so that the data with which they are working is both comprehensive and valid.

To Understand Spiritual and Religious Values

The schools of America have, since their inception, sidestepped spiritual and religious teachings in their curricula. Because of the premise that church and state be separated, schools have been legally bound to ignore the teaching of religion other than the minimal amount allowed by law. Spiritual and religious values are not necessarily the dogma of any specific religious creed. Spiritual and religious values, as we want them for our children, are the concepts of the brotherhood of man and the time tried ethics of the human race. Our children need these values.

Because we have grown secure in the belief that church and state are separate entities in America we can become more liberal in our views toward the teaching of moral and religious principles in our schools. We want our children to learn the customs of our group and we want them to know our values which are in great part customs which contribute to the growth of the group. We don't want our children to be taught a specific brand of religion but we want them to survey religious thought and to understand and use the time tried moral concepts therein which are in great part universal to all religions.

To Think as a Free Man

We want our children to be able to think. We want them to think independently and we want them to think fearlessly. We want our children to think logically and with integrity. We want them to reach sound conclusions and we want them to stand by their conclusions with strength. We want our children to be able to think rationally about all things. We want them to do so with a free conscience. We must teach children how to think through the content which the school and the home provide. Upon leaving school we want our children to think about anything which they choose as free men in our culture, utilizing the methods of logic which they mastered in their growth to adulthood.

To Practice Worthy Use of Leisure Time

Each succeeding decade provides more leisure time for the people of America. The production of our goods and services requires fewer man-hours per unit than were formerly required. The management of the home has also been made less laborious and time consuming by modern technology. Each decade sees an increase in the amount of leisure time given to the people of our nation and each decade also sees an increase in the amount of unexpended energy in each person. We must give to our children healthy avenues for the use of this leisure time and for the expenditure of their energies which will make a contribution to the growth of the individual and of the national community. We must teach our children how to deal with modern amusements such as television. We must teach them how to use them to their advantage and to enrich their lives rather than to restrict their lives. We want our children to enjoy the amusement aspects of modern technology in a balanced fashion. We want them to participate in both active and passive amusement in a healthy fashion. We want them to change the present trend of spectator entertainment to more involved and participating entertainment.

To Be Healthfully Self-expressive

Self-expression has fallen into disrepute. What was originally defined as self-expression has in many instances become license. America is reacting violently to the latter definition of self-expression.

Our national community will survive only if we have healthfully self-expressive citizens. Healthful self-expression is expression which does not interfere with the rights and freedom of others. When it does interfere it becomes unhealthy both for the individual and the group. The intra-freedom of democracy is a difficult balance to achieve. It is the balance between the expressive needs of the individual and the organizational needs of the group. We want our children to fit into this balance happily. We want them to be self-expressive but we want them to be so in proper relation to the mores and needs of the culture.

These objectives are indigenous to our national community. They are the reflections of the needs of the members of the community who strive to be successful. Different communities will stress different objectives as dictated by the needs peculiar to that community. In addition to these universal objectives, each community and each family presents more local and more specific objectives. These must be added to the list above if the child is to be completely successful in his immediate environment.

The objectives above cannot be achieved *in toto* by children in the elementary school. They can be initiated and fostered by the elementary school and can be met in part by the elementary school child. All other social agencies working toward the improvement of individuals and the community must supplement the work of the elementary school and must continue that work toward as complete achievement of these objectives as is possible.

CHAPTER III

Educational Methods

How Will They Teach?

Educational methods reflect the educational philosophy under which they operate. In so doing, they reflect both the strengths and weaknesses of that philosophy. The following descriptions of present day educational methods reflect the evolution of the elementary school throughout the years and also reflect our more valid knowledge about children as derived from experience in education. Practice, however, lags behind theory, in most fields. The trends are in process and although both theory and practice are far from ideal, the educational profession is gradually coming closer to the ideal.

One of the most basic changes in method will be the stabilization of the present tendency to postpone the introduction of many academic skills. Such changes will be consolidated and the subject matter introduction will not be postponed for as long a period of time as it is at present.

Athletics

The main objective of the athletic program of the future will be the socialization of children. Gone will be the day when it was considered that a rigid diet of athletics and regulated calisthenics made a contribution to good health. We know from watching children at play that they exercise as many muscles equally as often in free play as they do in organized gymnastic exercises. Children profit from organized group games, however, in that they are learning to deal with social situations under rules through the give-and-take of being a team member and the give-and-take required in team against team competition. Another basic change in athletics will be the growth toward universality of participation. All children will be involved in the games. Children with a physical disability will be given comparable activities aimed at correcting the disability in so far as possible within the framework of the organization at the school. The day of competition for only the successful and the proficient child will be gone. Inter-school games will involve many teams playing at one time. These teams will be matched for proficiency but all teams will contribute toward the final scores and all children who are able will play.

Arithmetic

The teaching of arithmetic falls into three categories:

> a. Functional arithmetic
> b. Formal arithmetic
> c. Modern arithmetic

Those who subscribe to the first school of thought feel that we should learn only those arithmetic concepts which will be useful. They suggest that we eliminate such fractions as $1/9$ or $1/7$ from the arithmetic program because we rarely have measurement techniques which are calibrated to sevenths or ninths. They also feel that arithmetic should be learned in a useful context wherein a child learns to compute when he needs it. They suggest that the school set up activities the completion of which will require some form of computation. Having this need to do the required computation the child will be motivated to learn the computational method which will be presented by the teacher at that time. This philosophy is based on children's needs and motivation. It restricts the curriculum in that many computational needs which arise in activities are simple and do not cover the many facets of arithmetic which make for a thorough understanding of the function of numbers.

The adherents of the formal arithmetic school of thought feel that arithmetic is an organized discipline. They feel that it should be presented from the concrete to the abstract in an organized body. They feel that only through rigid methods will children be able to master the content of the arithmetic curriculum. They will also gain mental discipline through dealing with the computational problems presented to them. Those who favor this school of thought also feel that the elementary school is not a free agent, hence it must build a computational background for required work in mathematics at the secondary school and college levels.

The modern arithmetic adherents stress an understanding of the number system and of numeration as prime objectives. Within this system children are helped to "discover" arithmetic concepts. The rote learning of rules and techniques are not acceptable within this concept. Children are exposed to geometric and quantitative principles during the early elementary school years which were formerly reserved for the secondary school years. The content of modern arithmetic stresses such areas as systems, sets, numeration, algebraic equations and geometry during the first and second grade years. The modern arithmetic system is presently becoming the most accepted system for teaching arithmetic in our elementary schools.

The elementary school of the future must meet the quantitative needs of children under all of these systems. It must give children an organized background for dealing with the complexities of calculus, trigonometry and other quantitative studies because the secondary schools and colleges require them. It must also give children practice in using arithmetic in their daily lives when dealing with measurements, budgeting allowances and in many other practical situations. It must further begin to teach children to understand our number system and why we do what we do with it.

The arithmetic teacher must pool these three points of view and must make the study of formal arithmetic interesting and meaningful in addition to motivating the student through practical experiences with computational skills and number concepts which they are learning.

The Arts

The arts include such activities as the visual arts, painting, modeling, drawing, and other creative areas such as music, dancing, creative writing, and drama, etc. A synonym for the arts as used here is "creative activity."

Here lies one of the most profound extensions of the basic problem facing elementary education, the problem of technique versus expression. As with all forms of expression, we must decide which aspect we shall emphasize and at what time.

The problem will be easily solved in the visual arts. The visual arts program of the elementary school of the future will have as its primary objective expressions of the individual's inner feelings through creative expression. The school of the future will abolish art lessons which stress such techniques as perspective and camera type picture making and will substitute "art for fun." Art for fun will stress story telling, imaginative problems and the general satisfaction of the artist. The artist will be the most important factor, the viewer and the critic will be practically overlooked. This will also be the case with the teaching of the dance in the elementary school. In both instances, technique will be a very minute part of the instruction and evaluation will be made primarily on the basis of expressive content and the satisfaction of the creator.

Because expression in music is limited at an early level by lack of technique, it will be perused from the expressive point of view during the early years of the elementary school only. From the third grade on technique will assume a more important place in the teaching of music. Added, however, about this time will be the area of appreciation which will be a new form of musical study. Here technique is not nearly as important as satisfaction, hence the emphasis from this point on will be dual: expressive and technical.

The drama of the elementary school of the future will be almost entirely expressive in nature. Gone will be the era of choosing published plays and the memorization of lines for their production. The drama of the future will be written by children and acted in childlike fashion. The creation of the play and the involvement of the performers will be the most important factors in drama. The audience will be very secondary. Evaluation of dramatic activities will be made solely on the basis of their effect on the dramatists and not on their effect upon the audience.

Dancing will assume a new importance in the school of the future. Its primary objective will be creativity and self-expression. Folk dancing and creative dancing, both group and individual, will become an important facet of the elementary school program. Participation and expression will be the keynote with audience reaction and the training of the performers as secondary objectives.

The dance and music programs will become more inseparable as time goes by and the elementary school music will combine the two.

Creative Expression

Creative expression has been much maligned by the critics of the pregressive movement. The progressive movement rightly deserved much of this criticism for over the years it has abused and misused the concept of self- or creative expression.

The need for avenues of self-expression is obvious. All humans, children and adult, need outlets for the emotional energy which is suppressed in their daily lives. Emotional reactions which are accepted by our culture leave a great deal of the emotional force generated by a situation within the individual. For example: Although we have many daily experiences which arouse emotional reactions, we cannot give full vent to those emotions less we shock those around us or lose the status we have gained as good citizens. We therefore inhibit much of the emotional force generated until a more politic time for expression. This inhibited emotional force if unexpressed festers and is a causal factor in most instances of personality disorganization. It must be removed if we are to remain mentally healthy. We must seek avenues for the expression of this force which will not jeopardize our relations with our fellow man. Some of us become unduly upset if our dinner is not ready on time, or if a child knocks over a glass of water at the dinner table, as a form of expressing the emotional force which we inhibited during the day because we did not want to lose status with our co-workers. Those who are better adjusted tend to expend this energy in expressive and recreational activities.

The same process takes place with children. They store up a

tremendous amount of emotional force which they don't dare express in front of their classmates, teachers and parents. It has been found that the healthiest and most acceptable way to express these emotional forces is through creative expression which can consist of play, certain forms of agressive behavior, music, hobbies, art, competitive sports and so on. The school of the future will be cognizant of this need in children and will provide avenues for the expression of these emotional forces which will be acceptable to society at each developmental level. Young children will expend these energies through imaginative play, creative art, telling and acting out stories, and performing to music. Older children will add to these avenues creative writing, reading books which are therapeutic in nature, playing organized games, pursuing hobbies, and argumentative discussion.

The school of the future will give all children many opportunities to express these emotional energies. It will evaluate the above mentioned activities primarily relative to the amount of stored-up emotional force expended and will only secondarily evaluate the proficiency exhibited in the above media of expression.

Drill Activities

Repetition is a very necessary facet of learning. It must be varied and interesting. Too much drill of an unvaried nature is deadening to children's interests. Repetition of materials learned can be accomplished through many varied activities. Drill must be suited to the needs of the individuals in the class. The amount of repetition necessary for the mastery of a concept varies from child to child. The onus which drill has received is the result of the indiscriminate use of unvaried drill in the same amount for each child regardless of his own particular needs. The school of the future will use repetition as a necessary part of learning. Such repetition will be suited to the learning needs of each child and will be made as interesting as possible.

Foreign Languages

The teaching of foreign languages will begin in the earliest years of the elementary school as our foreign language needs become more obvious because of improved communication and transportation.

The present method of beginning the study of foreign languages in the Junior High School has as its objectives the knowledge of the language at a paper and pencil and analytical level. Studies indicate that equal children starting at that time and those beginning at the elementary school level make about the same scores on college entrance tests. These same studies indicate, however, that those children with the earlier training in a foreign language are better able to understand the language when it is spoken and can speak it more proficiently. As the need for speaking and understanding spoken language is made more urgent by our more rapid transportation and by our growing concept of international communication, the teaching of foreign languages in the elementary school will become a fairly universal practice.

This teaching will start at the first grade level with songs and interesting rote exercises in the language and will be made gradually more comprehensive as children move through the elementary school. Such a program merely awaits more impetus from a rapidly advancing transportation and communication technology and from the growing American attitude toward greater and greater interaction with other countries.

General Knowledge

The school of the future will spend much time in increasing the general knowledge of its students. It will do so as a reaction to the age of specialization. Elementary school children will be exposed to a very liberal education, for the specialist of the future will not be accepted solely on his specialized knowledge. He will be required to have a fund of general information in addition to his specialized information. As a reaction to our present, somewhat narrow, concept of specialization a premium will be put on broad general knowledge in addition to specialization. This trend toward a broader concept of education will permeate the elementary school which will in turn emphasize the importance of a broad fund of general knowledge.

History and Geography

The teaching of history and geography will have, in the future, the same starting points; the here-and-now of the child. The child's geography will start with himself, his home, and will move out from there. He will study about his community, then spread out until he has covered world geography. The emphasis will not be upon memorization of facts, but upon understanding inter-relationships of geography and culture and the understanding of the effect of geography upon the course of civilization and upon himself.

Simultaneously the child will be studying history. He will start with himself today and then go back in time and will also learn the history of his expanding geographic universe. The history of religions will be studied as a part of the study of the history of civilization.

Because of the egocentric tendency of all children, education will in the future begin with the here-and-now of the child and emanate from there in both time and space. Children will move away from themselves in their history and geography activities and in so doing will gain a healthy perspective of themselves, as they relate to their homes, their communities, their country and the world at large.

Hobby Clubs

Every child in the elementary school will have a choice of a hobby activity which he can pursue at least one session per week at school. Most schools will offer a choice of hobby activities such as these:

Archery	Metal Work
Art	Models
Automobiles	Movies
Brownies	Music
Camera	Photography
Ceramics	Radio
Cooking	Rifle
Cub Scouts	Sewing
Current Events	Sports
Gardening	Stamps
Jokes	Weaving
Library	Woodwork

Because of the increasing amount of leisure time being made available to our citizens, hobbies will become increasingly important in the school. They will not be considered extra-curricular but will be integrated into the program of the elementary school and will be continued in the secondary school as an integral facet of the curriculum.

Homework

Because many educators have questioned the value of homework at the elementary school level, most schools have dispensed with homework. The absence of homework assignments is the result of a somewhat narrow concept of the nature of homework and the somewhat narrow evaluation of its values. Because many professions require work at home and because colleges and most secondary schools require homework, children will eventually be faced with the need to work at home. There is evidence that certain types of homework activities are very valuable in establishing this ability to work in other places besides school or office. There is ample evidence that many types of homework activity are very valuable to children, even at the content level, during the third through sixth grade years.

The school of the future will begin to establish homework habits with pleasant tasks such as collecting pictures or objects, visiting community agencies and collecting interesting experiences of many sorts at the second grade level. The objective of these activities will be the establishment of an awareness of the responsibility to and value in homework through attractive and non-frustrating assignments. During the latter half of the elementary school years the assignments will incorporate the added objective of helping the child to fix the material learned through added use in different situations or through different media.

Homework will therefore be an integral part of the program of the elementary school of the future. It will not be the wholly drill type of activity as was used heretofore. It will be as interesting and non-frustrating as possible. It will include drill activities which are both varied and practical. It will be individualized so that it meets the needs of many students and it will give them many opportunities to be creative at an individual level.

Language

The language area includes all media of communication. Mass communication is a basic tenet of democracy. The language area, therefore, is crucial to the success of the school.

Because all sections of our nation speak the same language, our problem of teaching people to communicate orally is simplified. Most children arrive at school knowing how to converse with others. The teaching of oral language is primarily concerned with the development of greater vocabulary and the refinements of oral habits.

A relatively new area of teaching must be utilized in the teaching of listening. Children, if they are to be successful, must learn to listen efficiently and effectively. They must learn to listen critically and to be able to distinguish between truth and propaganda.

The teaching of spelling needs revision. These exists, at present, a dichotomy in method. One method stresses rote memory work and workbooks and the other stresses meeting spelling needs, i.e., we have to learn to spell those words we want to use in our writing. Teachers of spelling caught between these two schools of thought have tended to use portions of both and in so doing have slighted the area of spelling. Much less time is spent on spelling than formerly. Because of the lack of clarity of the methodology and because of the lack of time spent on spelling, spelling proficiency on the part of the students has declined. The school of the future must have a more clarified methodology, more personal teaching, with fewer workbooks, and more time spent on spelling if it is to meet the needs of the secondary schools, colleges, and industry.

The teaching of writing also needs clarification. One school of thought insists that writing begins with the formation of letters. From there it progresses to the writing of words, sentences, paragraphs and so on, studying at each level the rules which govern their composition. This theory states that when a child has mastered these mechanics he will be able to write and will be willing to use these techniques in expressing himself in written language. The antithesis contends that all writing must begin from motivation. This theory contends that the teaching of writing begins with discussions and activities which give children ideas for their writing. The next step is motivating them into wanting to write. Then the children with ideas to write about and the need to write will learn to form letters, to write sentences and paragraphs. The proponents of both theories hold that their method of teaching has distinct values. Both methods do. It is the task of the school of the future to combine the emphasis of mechanics and the emphasis of motivation in a balanced fashion wherein children will learn the mechanics of writing without losing the spontaneous willingness to write, or without disliking the expressive aspect of writing because of the difficulty in mastering the techniques.

The elementary school of the future must accept the most modern concepts and data in the teaching of reading. Not only must the elementary school of the future create even more superior readers than it does at present, it must prevent "reading problems." Reading problems are the basis of the greatest amount of criticism leveled at the elementary school. Reading problems are the basis of the most emotional and most violent criticism of the elementary school. The most significant changes in the teaching of reading in the future will be the following:

1. Reading will be taught earlier in the life of the child.
2. Reading methods will begin with teaching whole words and then move on to structural and phonetic analysis.
3. With the cooperation of the school and home reading problems can and will be prevented.

1. Modern experimentation has indicated that reading can be learned much earlier than had previously been assumed. In the past children who read very early in life were considered unique and extremely gifted. Such children are becoming increasingly commonplace. Babies are learning to read through modern methods of presenting large word cards to them under happy and successful circumstances. This experience of recognizing large symbols helps to sophisticate the visual pathways of the child. This early development coupled with early success helps the child

to be introduced to the reading process without pressure from other children and without fear of failure. The advantage so gained tends to be maintained throughout school.

New books and new materials for early reading are being published.[1] The advent of the early reader in the elementary and the preschool will make mandatory new techniques for teaching reading. These early readers will also make it necessary to establish new norms for reading success. What is considered good reading performance today will be mediocre in the future.

2. The increased goals for the modern reader make it mandatory that we begin the teaching of reading with the whole method. Those children who learn by the whole method always remain the best readers in their groups. For those who cannot learn by the whole method a more analytic method must be used. These children never achieve the superior goals in reading achieved by children who learn by the whole method.

The elementary school of the future will begin the teaching of reading with the whole or word sight method. In this method the children are merely told what the word is and a memory process is used to master a basic vocabulary.

As this basic vocabulary of one to two hundred words is mastered (memorized) the most facile children begin to develop their own systems for attacking new words. In a typical middle class community approximately 35 to 50 per cent of the pupils can master reading in this fashion. These children go on to achieve the highest goals in reading. They always hold the advantage gained through not needing to be encumbered by unnecessary cues to word recognition.

The remaining children must be taught other cues to word recognition. They cannot learn to read through the memory method. They need structural cues (i.e., finding small words in large words) and phonetic cues (i.e., learning the sounds of the letters and the letter combinations). This group never achieves the ultimate excellence in reading skills that is achieved by the sight group. Since they cannot learn to read adequately without added cues they must be taught such cues.

The present obvious errors in technique will soon be alleviated.

---

[1]Doman, G.: *Teach Your Baby to Read:* Random House, New York, 1964. Materials are published by Systems for Education, 612 North Michigan Avenue, Chicago, Ill.

They are the result of parent and teacher groups who are determined to prove that one method is right for all children. These errors fall into two groups:

a. Schools which are so wed to the sight method that even when they have achieved the success expected with the sight group insist that the remainder of the group learn by sight when it is obvious that they cannot.

b. Schools which are so wed to the phonetic method that they insist that all children learn by the phonetic system from the outset even though they know that 35 to 50 per cent of the group do not need phonetics and that indeed the teaching of phonetics at this stage will hamper these children in their efforts to achieve excellence in ultimate reading performance.

The obvious compromise will be to siphon off from the group the children who learn by sight alone through using the whole word method at the outset. When this has been done the remainder of the children must be taught structural and phonetic analysis if they are to learn to read.

3. Reading problems can be prevented. Modern experimentation has shown us that most reading problems are reading problems long before they enter school. The prevention of reading problems must take place at home. We must first of all understand how most of our reading problems are developed in order to understand how they can be prevented.

The Ontogeny of Reading Problems[2]

The title, "The Ontogeny of Reading Problems," is I am sure, somewhat surprising. Instead of this title, we could entitle this, "The Development of a Reading Problem." We, in the field of the language arts, have spent our greatest efforts in attempts to ameliorate such problems and it is my purpose here to discuss with you the development of such problems. Perhaps, viewing our language problems from this point of view might give us a somewhat different form of insight into the types of problems which we encounter with children who are disabled in some phase of language and communication functions.

We would all agree that reading is a developmental process. I

[2]Delacato, C. H., from the *Proceedings of the Claremont Reading Conference*, Claremont, California, January, 1963.

am sure that we would all agree that reading is basically a receptive act, that it consists primarily of visual reception and, at some levels, auditory reception and perhaps kinaesthetic reception are involved. We also know that we, as educators and as a reflection of a culture, *measure* the proficiency with which a human being deals with the process called reading, via expressive modalities. We, therefore, measure what is basically a receptive act by its expressive concomitants.

If we follow this sequentially, we have the fact that the reading process is basically *receptive* and that we measure the effectiveness of the reading process primarily *expressively*. If one, therefore, has difficulty with the reading process, we know that he has difficulty with it because he lacks expressively, since we measure his function via an expressive modality.

Carried one step further, we ascertain the aggregate expressive distillate of the perceptual processes of reading. We evaluate the *percepts* by measuring and evaluating the *concepts* formed on the basis of those perceptual skills.

In the past we have confused the process of learning and of the mastery of communication skills by going from concept, which we use as our measuring technique, back to percept. We must all agree that logically we develop perceptually and then move on to concept in the development of language abilities.

The great majority of our reading problems are receptive problems. They are problems of perception. We find that, even those children suffering from a lack of comprehension, which certainly indicates a conceptual lack, are suffering, not from conceptual problems, but from perceptual problems. When we give such children instructions orally we find that they can understand and comprehend and conceptualize the same words and sentences which they cannot comprehend and conceptualize via reading. Our natural conclusion must be that this is the result of poor percepts on which they are basing their resulting inadequate concepts.

Receptive problems are the result of faulty or incomplete neurological organization. These problems are created long before we, as educators, ever see the children. These perceptive problems can be diagnosed long before we generally see children in our pre-schools. These problems can be treated long before we, as educators, see them in our schools. Finally, these problems can be prevented.

A lack of adequate neurological organization can be the result of a genetic bias. This represents a very small percentage of our problems in the typical schools of America. A second area of etiology is a trauma. This again is a small percentage of our population. The third etiological area is the area of lack of environmental opportunity for complete neurological organization. This group represents by far the greatest majority of our problems in the area of communication.

Diagnostically we can begin to assess the etiology of such problems prior to birth. A family history helps to give us an insight into the existence of that small group which is potentially genetic in etiology. Birth data of early childhood illness and trauma give us an insight into the second small group, the group which is the result of a traumatic etiology.

The third and by far the largest group (that group which is the result of environmental deprivation) can be seen if we view the child in sequential stages from a developmental and functional neurological bias.

For our purposes of looking at the development of a reading problem, let us look at this largest group. Let us look at the significant stages of development to see how the lack of opportunity for complete neurological organization at each successive stage of neurological development relates to the ontogeny of a reading problem. For our purposes, let us look at the successive stages receptively in terms of audition and vision and expressively in terms of movement.

As the child who has had a non-traumatic birth arrives at three to twenty weeks of age we find that his mobility consists of crawling on his stomach in a homolateral pattern. That is, the child moves forward with the arm and leg on the same side of the body extended and the arm and leg on the opposite side of the body flexed. His head turns toward the flexed side and as he moves, this body position is reversed. The mobility is aimed in a two-dimensional world toward seeking vital and basically crude comfort. If we view the child at this age from a visual point of view, we note that his body position places his eyes in such a position that he is *biocular* in visual performance. That is, as his right arm and leg come up his right eye looks at the right hand, the left eye does not. It remains somewhat strabismic. As the position is reversed, the left eye looks at the left hand and the right eye has no part in the visual process. At this stage the child operates visually *biocularly,* using only one eye at a time, just as he uses one side of his body at a time in the homolateral pattern.[3]

The same is true in audition. At this stage the child cannot place sound in space simply because auditorially he receives the stimulus from one ear or the other. This total performance lies in terms of neurological organization at the level of pons. This is basically a one-sided level of function. Mobility is *homolateral,* or one side used for propulsion at a time, vision is biocular, audition is *biaural.*

When the child moves on to the level of mid-brain at the age of seven to nine months, we find a whole new area of function arising. The child, in terms of mobility, adds the third dimension to his movement. He now creeps on his hands and knees and his stomach is no longer in contact with the floor. Significantly, as he moves now, the opposite appendages are used for propulsion. In other words, as he moves, the right hand and left knee are used at one time and then the left hand and right knee are used for propulsion. The child has now become a cross-patterned organism. He no longer is one-sided, but now is distinctly two-sided. He becomes a *bilateral* human being.

In vision, at this stage, he begins to use his eyes in concert. He no longer uses one eye at a time in a biocular fashion. Instead, he uses his two eyes in concert and here is the beginning of *binocularity.* Those children who present to us later in the developmental picture a lack of good binocularity are children who have not been given adequate opportunity to develop binocularity at this stage of development, which is the responsibility of midbrain. Such children, who are not given adequate opportunities for creeping, later develop problems in which binocularity is a variable.

[3]Delacato, C. H.: *The Treatment and Prevention of Reading Problems.* Thomas, Springfield, 1959.

In audition the same phenomenon takes place at the level of mid-brain. During the seven to nine month developmental level the child learns to place sound in space. He becomes *binaural,* that is, he now tends to use his two ears in concert. The stimulae are mediated and the child can place a sound in space.

We have all seen these children to whom we could not teach phonetics, no matter how hard we tried. In our investigations we find that those children are lacking in this very basic binaural skill, which is the function of mid-brain and not of the cortex, as we had assumed in the past. Children who are not afforded the opportunities for development at the level of mid-brain in the area of vision, mobility and audition at the ages of seven to nine months are beginning to develop significant problems in communication. If they lack binocularity, binaural function and mid-brain overall responsiveness, we have started them on their way toward a disability in language.

As children reach one year of age they become cortical creatures and they move from bilateral activity, binocular activity and binaural activity to a new level of function, that is stereo or depth within their receptive and expressive mobilities. Children from the age of one on begin to develop *stereopsis* in vision. This must be superimposed upon strong binocularity. They begin to develop *stereophonic* abilities in hearing which must be superimposed upon strong binaural abilities. They begin to develop true *cross-pattern walking,* which must be superimposed upon the more elemental midbrain cross-pattern creeping. Indeed, at this time in the other areas of receptiveness they have developed from the level of pons, at which they were able to receptively discriminate between very painful and very strong stimuli along to the point at the level of cortex wherein they have developed complete *stereognosis* receptively.

In a few short years from birth the child has moved from being one-sided to being two-sided: binocularly, binaurally and bilaterally, to being stereophonic, having developed stereopsis, having developed stereognosis and now must move on to the final human level, that of developing or superimposing upon this developmental continuum *cortical hemispheric dominance.* Here is where man is unique in neurological terms. Man is the only creature who has developed one hemisphere which is dominant over the other hemisphere. As a result, man is the only creature who has a symbolic language.[4]

As a child begins to make early choices of sidedness, the culture must give him opportunities to reinforce this sidedness so that he develops complete unilaterality, which results in one-sidedness for *handedness, footedness* and *eyedness*. As he develops complete one-sidedness, he can begin the process of becoming completely human in terms of his receptive and expressive abilities.

This sequential continuum, called neurological organization, ends at about the age of six, or at about the age when we generally begin to teach reading formally. To recapitulate, the whole process of development of readiness to read begins at birth. It goes on to the level of pons, which functions in an alternating one-sidedness, to the level of mid-brain, which is two-sidedness, to the level of cortex, which encompasses stereo functions, to the level of the development of complete cortical hemispheric dominance. This continuum forms the basis of human perceptual abilities.

Perception is a fundamental process. We learn to see in varying stages and in varying ways; we learn to move in varying stages and varying ways; we learn to hear in varying stages and varying ways; we learn to feel in varying stages and varying ways. There are no short cuts to these developmental processes in any of the sensory modalities, sequentially, logically and according to the development of the human nervous system. Only by going through the process as nature meant it to be can we form good perceptual abilities.

Superimposed upon the development of perceptual abilities are the apperceptions which we build from our experiences which, in turn, result in conceptualization and the ultimate in reading, which is human conceptual comprehension. The ability to learn to read, the ability to learn to express oneself starts from birth on. If one is not afforded the opportunity to develop this total neurological organization, he cannot become totally human, and as a result, cannot communicate at the level at which he might

---

[4]Delacato, C. H.: *The Diagnosis and Treatment of Speech and Reading Problems.* Thomas, Springfield, 1963.

have been able to had his neurological organization been complete.

To diagnose our language problems, therefore, we must start at the age at which we first see the child, but we must look back developmentally to the original area of dysfunction. As a result, it may be that in terms of diagnosis, some of our children are not well developed at the level of pons, some at the level of mid-brain, some at the level of cortex and some at the level of cortical hemispheric dominance. If we are to diagnose validly and reliably, we must go through each succeeding stage to assess the mastery) of function at each stage.

Treatment must also follow this sequence. In treatment we must go back to the original point of departure from developmental norms and we must re-create for that brain level and that chronological level those functions so that the child can go through the proper developmental stages and begin to move on to the establishment of complete neurological organization. In treatment, therefore, we must start at the lowest level at which there appears to be a lack of neurological organization and we must give the child the opportunity to master the activities and functions of that level and of each succeeding level until we have mastered complete cortical hemispheric dominance.

Based on the rationale of neurological organization, prevention of communication dysfunction is very possible. It must be based, however, on the premise that there are *significant* developmental stages of neurological organization which cannot be bypassed, and as the child reaches each stage chronologically he must be given every opportunity to master the functional neurological activities at that level before moving on to the next. With such a logical approach to child education we could, in the future, become able to prevent the problems which face us in education today by seeing that every child is given opportunity to develop wholly and completely in terms of functional neurological organization.

Literature

Children's literature of the future will be quite different from that of the past and that of the present. Their literature in the past consisted of a small number of literary "classics" which were read first by parents to children, then were reread by the children when they were able to cope with the vocabulary. Most of the content of these classics was assimilated by the children when they first heard the books read. Reading the books on the part of children became merely the mastery of word recognition and a review of content with which they were thoroughly familiar. Such a system for the introduction of literature exposed children to a literature of good quality but also made it a literature which lacked breadth and was basically repetitive and unstimulating.

The present literature for children follows somewhat the same pattern. It consists primarily of literary works which adults feel should be good children's literature. The most basic changes have been in format, pictures and general attractiveness of books. The content is still tuned, however, toward what publishing houses feel parents will buy for their children, not what children might choose to read for themselves. Marketability, therefore, has been the primary criterion of the quality of the literature for children.

Children have reacted to this lack of good literature which really meets their needs by reading what is considered in most part poor literature; or by not reading anything.

As suitable materials are published, children will read it. Such materials must be of good quality and must be well written at proper vocabulary level. These materials cannot be written "down" to children but must be written "for" them. They must be interesting enough to compete with the many interesting activities available to the modern child and must be interesting enough to compete with many other fascinating recreational media. Above all, the new literature must be written by those who have great insight into the modern concept of children's understandings and feelings. Such a body of literature will not only make for the reading of material of better quality but will also make for more reading and for more proficient reading on the part of children.

Manual Arts Program

The objectives of the manual arts program will be identical for both boys and girls. They will be:

Learning to use simple hand tools effectively.
Learning the rudiments of simple home maintenance.

Learning to use simple hand tools effectively will be done by both sexes. Both boys and girls will be involved with the same projects, the completion of which will give them a working knowledge of simple hand tools. In addition to the project work which will be of relatively free choice, both boys and girls will be given periodic explanations and practice in the rudiments and principles of simple home maintenance. Tasks such as repairing electric outlets, putting washers in faucets and repairing slightly damaged furniture and such other repair type tasks which constantly arise in the typical home will be explained and assigned to each child.

The Junior High School program will be an extension of the manual arts program into shop work for the boys and the inclusion of domestic science training for the girls. At the ninth grade level girls and boys will exchange shop and home economics periods for nine weeks per year and will continue to do so through the tenth grade.

The manual arts program and its extension into shop and home economics with a turn-about program in the ninth and tenth grades will tend to educate students toward making a real contribution to family living and toward real cooperation at a family level.

Mental Health

The critical need for a sound approach to mental health has been and still is the most dramatic educational problem of this century. It will become an even more critical problem during the last half of this century. The tempo of modern American life coupled with its increasing complexity make a sound program of mental health in our schools mandatory. These factors, which are causal in the realm of poor mental health, will increase with time and their potential toward increasing personality disorganization will do likewise. Unless the schools accept this challenge and unless every social institution allies itself with the school in this area the resultant waste of human and financial resources may become disastrous in nature.

The school of the future will be very involved with the attitudes and feelings of children. It will constantly attempt in all of its activities to foster healthy attitudes and will constantly be cognizant of the feelings of children. The objectives of the school and the methods used to achieve them will be used only in light of the experimentally demonstrated principles of the best mental hygiene. Teaching and teachers which do not make for healthy attitudes on the part of children will be eliminated in the school of the future.

Motivation

Helping children to want to learn is a relatively new idea in the history of education. It is one of the most profound contributions to education made by the progressive movement. The insight into human personality and into human motives has increased tremendously since the beginning of this century. Its practical application in school situations has also made tremendous strides. The weakest strain of logic in the movement was fostered by those who did not understand the processes whereby good motivation was fostered. This group assumed that good motivation meant teaching children only what they wanted to learn. This was true, but minimal. It has been demonstrated that children can be motivated to learn in areas in which they have no innate or natural interest under the guidance of good teachers.

The area of motivation, therefore, has shifted from teaching children what they should know without motivating them to teaching them only what they want to know. The school of the future, through good teachers who present learning materials interestingly and effectively, will help children to want to learn about the things which they should learn if they are to be successful in our culture.

Musical Organizations

For those children who have better than average musical talents and training, elective membership in musical organizations, both vocal and instrumental, will be available. These organizations will increase the importance of audience reaction and quality of performance and will strive for proficient execution within the framework of the capacities and training of the students.

Play

"The higher the level of animals, the greater portion of their lives is spent in childhood play" is a premise which is easily observed. Human beings need a longer period of early play than does any other animal.

Play falls into two caterogies, free and organized. Young children prefer free play wherein they dictate the form and content of the play activities. Such play is usually imaginative and through it children give vent to many inner tensions and to many of their feelings. Very young children prefer to play alone. As they grow they feel the necessity to play with others maintaining, however, the free type of play. Following this social type of free play children begin to need organization or rules in their play, hence they move on to games which most children play such as hide-and-seek, hop scotch and tag. This stage is followed by the need for continued social games at a group versus group level which is characteristic of most adult group games. Such games contain the element of competition within the group and group versus group competition. This type of play helps the individual to learn group action and the relation of one's ego to it, and helps the individual to see the group with which he is cooperating both win and lose. Such group competition fills a universal need toward the development of a full personality which is prepared to cope understandingly with the problems of a complex culture which emphasizes group living.

Practical Knowledge

Children will be given more information at an earlier age about how to deal with their immediate environment of people and things. They will be taught the basic premises of human interaction and will be sensitized to the people around them. This information will deal with family interactions and social interactions at a community level, in addition to the immediate value structure of the community.

They will also be taught how to deal with an ever more complex daily culture. They will be taught the problem areas of their physical surroundings and will learn to deal with the practical aspects of such things as budgeting, traffic safety, buying, community laws and many more areas of community environment. More school time will be spent in preparing children to assume the duties and privileges of community life.

Projects

Projects and project work have been much maligned in education. They are viewed by a larger portion of the populace than educators care to think as "time spent in meaningless play which could be better spent on learning the three R's." Such criticism is true of much of the transitional project-type teaching. It is not true, however, of project work which is aimed at those educational objectives which only that type of activity can meet. Project work must be the result of children's interests as an adjunct to the aspect of the program being pursued at the moment. Such work must be tuned toward a set of teacher-pupil objectives and must contain much of the learning-by-doing type of activity. This content will in most part be measurable as will the children's growth toward their objectives. Teachers and pupils will evaluate all projects relative to content mastered and relative to the objectives of the activity.

Safety Patrol

The primary objective of the Safety Patrol will be to educate as many children as possible in the rules of traffic safety. The members of the Safety Patrol will be involved with the regulation of both pedestrian and vehicular traffic under the personal supervision of local traffic officials. They will arrange for moving pictures, lectures and many other educational activities dealing with traffic safety. They will also be in charge of posting pictures and exhibits stressing safety throughout the school. They will be called upon for help in relieving all types of student traffic on the school grounds. Membership in the Safety Patrol will be voluntary on the part of the children. They will become eligible at the fifth grade level.

School Paper

All elementary school children will be given the opportunity to contribute to the school paper. Standards for the acceptance of such materials for publication in the school paper will vary with the age levels of the authors. The objective of the newspaper staff will be the publication of the creative expression of all age levels from as many different individuals as possible. Gone will be the school newspaper which was a quasi-perfect mimic of adult publications. Such a change in philosophy will eliminate the typical school newspaper which is stereotyped and in most instances trite. It will result in school publications which are rich in expressive content and which are truly representative of the creative techniques, attitudes and expressive forms of the student body.

School Store

Children of the latter years of the elementary school will plan and execute the activities of the school store. Classroom groups will rotate the responsibility for the store. They will order, store, sell, advertize and keep all of the accounts for the project, both as a learning activity and as a cooperative civic endeavor.

Science

The science program of the school of the future will have the following two objectives:

Teaching of scientific facts and principles.
Teaching the scientific method.

Both of these objectives will be constantly and simultaneously striven for in the school of the future. Much of today's emphasis in science is on the mastery of facts. Many schools are gradually adding scientific principles. Both facts and principles should be end results of scientific observation. They should both represent the academic knowledge to be gained from the study of science. The school of the future must, in addition to increasing the child's scientific knowledge, provide the methodology for gathering further scientific data and must provide the emotional atmosphere which will continue to motivate the child toward seeking scientific data on his own. The method of observation plus the techniques of handling data at each successive developmental level must be taught to children if they are to continue to maintain interest and success in the area of science.

The emphasis of science during the early elementary school years will be upon the scientific method. Science lessons will be informal, arising out of the children's immediate environment. Textbooks will be non-existent at this level although references to texts will be abundant. The children's natural curiosity will be channelled and expanded upon and their observational methods will become more logical. The teaching of the scientific method will be informal and will be constantly ajusted to the maturity and interest levels of the children.

Ten and eleven year olds will be given a more formal experience in science. At this level the scientific method will be more intellectualized and verbalized by the children. A logical recapitulation of the scientific facts and principles learned during the early years will take place at this level. A number of excellent recapitulation-type texts will be available to teachers and most children will be provided with a science text book of this sort during a portion of the later years of the elementary school. The use of the books, however, will depend upon the needs of the children and the ability and training of the teacher in the field of science.

The basic change in the teaching of science will be the great additional emphasis on "science-mindedness" on the part of the children, the continuation of interest in science and the more logical use of observational data on the part of the people who have been taught by the new method.

Self-evaluation

Children will be taught to evaluate their own and other's activities. They will cooperatively evaluate the work of the group and of individuals relative to improvement over past performances under the guidance of the teacher. They will learn to establish valid criteria for success in tasks attempted. They will also learn to evaluate their own work as validly as possible. They will learn to be sympathetic toward human frailties yet maintain realistic concepts of success for themselves and others. Self-evaluation at a valid level requires an attitude of confidence and security. These feelings of confidence and security which are pre-requisite to realistic self-evaluation must be fostered by long-term satisfying group membership. A background of happy group experiences will enable children to honestly evaluate their performance in a realistic and healthy fashion. Such experiences will include many opportunities for self-evaluation on the part of the children in an understanding and sympathetic, yet realistic, school environment.

Sex Education

Because of the puritanic strain of logic prevalant in America we have gone through the following stages in sex education. The first was the absence of sex-education in any bona-fide form. The second has been growing since the beginning of World War II and forces sex education at all, whether or not they are ready for it or interested in it. From the total lack of sex-education to its over emphasis in school we again see the conservative—liberal friction in our schools.

The school of the future will be realistic about sex-education. It will teach sex-education to children when they are ready for it. It will not force sexual knowledge on children who are not ready to assimilate it. It will not try to achieve the label of "liberal" merely because all children beyond a certain age know the facts of life. Readiness for sex education varies just as does reading readiness and readiness for arithemitic, hence it should be taught when readiness is present.

Social Studies

The social studies area of the elementary school is a new and a greatly confusing area to teachers, students, and parents. There is no apparent agreement as to the purpose of teaching social studies. Here are some reasons which are in effect at present.

1. Social studies are a method of teaching history and geography

facts in a pleasant way. They also provide a logical association of places and events which are not provided when history and geography are taught as separate subjects.

2. Social studies are really exercises in social living. They provide activities wherein children learn to plan and to work together. Children learn through these activities to subjugate their egos to the will and needs of the group. Other learnings are incidental and secondary.

3. Social studies provide the cohesive "center of interest" which gives meaning to the unrelated aspects of the curriculum. In so doing, they furnish the "interest" factor which increases motivation. The other functions of social studies are secondary.

4. Social studies provide research and learning techniques which are constantly used in the study of areas of the culture. The mastery of these techniques is of prime importance and the content learned through them is of secondary and incidental importance.

These four divergent philosophies must be unified if social studies are to make the important contributions which it was hoped they would make when introduced.

It is possible to fuse these four points of view but the school of the future must do so in light of the needs of the community and, hence, the children. Each school must ascertain the needs of its community and its pupils and base its social studies emphasis upon that information. The needs of the community and the needs of the pupils must dictate the emphasis of the social studies at any given time.

The over-all view of the program must include at certain developmental levels each of these definitions above as the emphasized area.

The early period of elementary education must use the social living emphasis of social studies. During the kindergarten and first grade years, much time must be spent in helping children to learn to live together and to work together effectively and happily.

During the second and third grade years, social studies will add the center-of-interest aspect of the definition. During these years social studies will serve as the cohesion in the program. It will serve to give meaning to the various experiences in the program and will tend to help children to relate the various phases of their studies. Also introduced at this time will be the techniques of research.

From the fourth grade level all four aspects of social studies will be used but emphasis will be placed primarily on content and method of research.

The school of the future will spend more time on the history and geography aspects of social studies than it does at present. This will be in most part the result of pressure from the lower secondary school for more content mastery in these areas.

Trips

Children will take many trips to points of interest in the future. Such trips will be preceded by a study of the place or things to be visited. The study will be followed by making a list of objectives for the trip on the part of the children. The children, upon leaving for the trip, will have a background of information on what they are visiting and a list of objectives or things to look for. Upon their return from the trip the children will orally review their objectives and discuss their findings. Too many present day school trips are followed with the assignment, "Write about the Trip." Children in the future will write prior to the trip and discuss following it.

Trips will be taken to increase the background of knowledge of the children. They will be in most cases part of the general topic being studied in social studies. Trips will be taken to the community in all the areas studied by children and will also be taken to areas outside the community which can contribute to the children's growth.

Children of all ages will take trips. Seeing at first hand what they have been studying will increase the effectiveness of the teaching and will familiarize children with their community and its great relationship to the things taught in school.

Workbooks

Workbooks were originally introduced to the schools as drill exercises and busy work. They were somewhat indiscriminately assigned to pupils so that the teacher could pursue other activities while the children were completing workbook assignments. This was especially true in the multi-graded school.

The reaction of the progressives to workbooks was adamant and vociferous. They did not consider workbooks suitable educational material. Workbooks were considered too restrictive to teachers and harmful to the attitudes of children toward educational activities. Much of the criticism of workbooks was valid. They had become a standard piece of educational equipment for practically every course of study. Their format and composition were dictating the teaching procedures and the content of education in many schools.

The use of workbooks in the future will be moderate. They will be chosen and used by teachers and administrators who are thoroughly aware of their values and limitations. Their greatest value and use will be in the area of children's specific weaknesses. If used wisely and for specific purposes workbooks can make an important contribution to education. Workbooks will never replace good teaching nor will they in the future be used as "busy work." As the stigma attached to workbooks by the progressives diminishes, they will be used more universally in those situations wherein they can make a contribution to the program. They will never, however, regain their general acceptance of a number of years ago when each child was given a workbook for each subject area. The child of the future will never have more than two workbooks in a single academic year unless he has a specific disability at which the workbook is aimed.

Work Habits

Children will learn good work habits in the school of the future. Their activities will be goal directed and when completed, evaluated relative to their goals. Today's schools are criticized constantly for not providing ample opportunities for the development of good work habits. Much of this criticism is justified for many classroom programs are guided by the capricious interests of children or by the teacher-made goals which are unknown or resisted by the children.

Children will, in the future, be a very important factor in planning the work of the group. They will help to formulate their plans in light of the goals of the activities involved. They will be involved in the evaluation of their growth toward those goals. Such activities are prerequisite to good work habits and they are basic to learning.

Children will be taught the methods of achieving their objectives efficiently and will, in so doing, learn to organize their activities and learn to attack their assignments. They will learn to work consistently and will learn to persevere until the task has been completed. They will learn to evaluate the completed task and will learn to judge the quality of the work involved. The school of the future will be very concerned with the work habits of its students and will spend much time in the cultivation of good work habits and a healthy attitude toward good work habits.

Working Together

The student government at the elementary school level will not be a representative democracy. Such a government requires understandings which are beyond the students and takes from them the opportunity to learn at first hand the lessons of democracy. Student governments in the future will be examples of pure democracy at work. It will be of a town meeting nature with grades 1, 2, and 3, meeting at one time and grades 4, 5, and 6, meeting at another. A teacher will be the moderator and the children will bring to the meetings any problems which they feel are important.

* * * * * * *

Although none of the specific changes in teaching method indicated above is of an extreme nature, the composite result of these changes will alter the daily lives of elementary school children considerably. These specific changes in technique when generalized indicate a definite trend toward a more functional educational structure which is becoming more sharply tuned to more of the needs of the individual and of the community.

CHAPTER IV

Discipline

Will They Teach Children How to Behave?

The elementary school of the future will deal with discipline in the most modern way. The end result of all disciplinary training must be self-discipline. This is a point which no educator or parent will dispute. What then is the method for achieving this highly elusive self-discipline?

Present methods of teaching self-discipline range from a "laissez-faire" to a complete subjugation of the child. This is one of the most criticized areas of elementary education and of parenthood. The pendulum of method swings in many directions in attempting to cope with the problem of discipline.

Discipline is learned through the dynamics of the interaction between the organism and its frame of reference. If there are no such interactions there is very little learning. For example let us look at the average home and the children's use of the living room.

Home A—The children are not allowed to use the living room unless an adult is present. When using the living room the adult constantly re-emphasizes the rules in operation and the children have to follow them. When the adult in charge leaves the living room, the children also have to leave.

There is very little learning occurring in this situation. There is no interaction and the children are constantly "told" what to do and what not to do. There is very little growth of the "self" aspect of the "self-discipline" point of view.

Home B—The children are given free reign in the living room, anything they do is acceptable.

This type of situation does not offer a frame of reference within which to grow. Because there are no rules children cannot learn self-discipline because the situation requires no discipline.

In type A we have very little growth of "self" and in type B we have very little "discipline."

The school of the future must provide both facets of self-discipline for children if it is to meet their needs. It must give children restrictions and help them to live within those restrictions.

The concept of discipline is cultural. It reflects the level at which the culture is operating. The more complex the organism, the more time it spends in play in its early life. Man is the most complex member of the animal kingdom, hence its young spends the most time at play in its youth. The changeover from play to work and the acceptance of the rules of the culture are disciplines which must be mastered if the organism is to make a proper adjustment to its environment.

Within the framework of the culture many other transitional factors are operative toward giving a group its standards for behavior. For example:

> Gross group dislocations
> Personal adjustment environment

Gross group dislocations are those variations within the cultural frame of reference which are operative relative to the group's concept of discipline.

During the early 1930's we had such a dislocation which was financial in nature. During that time the birth rate went down and the size of families decreased in the middle class. The concept of child raising for the middle class was modified. During that period the rules for child raising became more stringent. Timed feedings, bottle feeding and stimulus-response types of training were in vogue at that time. Discipline for the middle class became more rigid. As the late thirties approached and the economy became more stable a looser type of discipline was accepted by the middle class. This gross process occurs at all levels of the culture and from all types of dislocations. There are some educational philosophers who feel that these gross dislocations are responsible for setting the pendulum of educational philosophy in motion and for keeping it in motion.

Problems of personal adjustment are also important.

One's evaluation of assertion and conformance on the part of children is in great part biased by one's background of experience and feeling at the moment. Our reactions to a situation are therefore colored by our own personality adjustment. We must strive toward a well adjusted group of teachers and parents if children's behavior is to be evaluated validly.

The discipline of the future can be generalized as follows: (See table on page 51.

If discipline is defined as the amount of adult control and supervision forced on the child to secure conformance we can plot the use of discipline on a graph. The former discipline curve is represented by the broken line. The future disciplinary situation is the type represented in the table by the black line. Here the amount of direction by adults is least during the earliest years of life. As the child becomes older and more nearly ready for school he must conform to a greater degree if he is to be happy. During the elementary school years he will have to learn to conform to the rules of the culture in which he lives, these rules being both individual and group.

Upon his mastery of the reason behind each guiding tenet and upon his acceptance of the tenet the child should be given the freedom to use it. As he develops through the elementary school years the child will be constantly introduced to new disciplines and rules set up by the culture. His acceptance of those rules indicates growth. Hence during these years, although the amount of direction is somewhat constant, the areas in which direction takes place is constantly changing as mastery and acceptance takes place.

A number of differences are represented by the two lines on the graph. The broken line indicates that children are introduced to disciplines at birth. These disciplines include such items as timed feedings and a regimented daily schedule. The discipline of the future will introduce these factors at a later age. The adult supervision of the future will reach its maximum at an earlier level than it did in the past but it will never quite reach the intensity of adult supervision that was reached in the past. The amount of adult supervision in the future will drop sharply from age twelve as indicated by the black line on the graph. It will cease during the late teens. The broken line indicates that under the former disciplinary pattern supervision decreased more slowly and that quite a bit of supervision was maintained until the child legally became an adult.

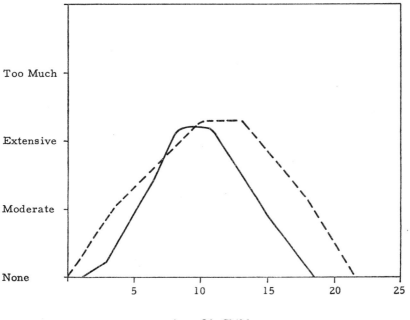

Amount of Adult Supervision

At Various Age Levels

Amount of
Supervision

Too Much

Extensive

Moderate

None

5   10   15   20   25

Age Of Children

▬ ▬ ▬ Former Method

▬▬▬ Future Method

The basic change in the disciplinary pattern of the future, as pictured in the graph will be that adult control will begin later in the child's life, it will accelerate and reach its peak sooner, will then decrease sharply and will be completely eliminated during the late teens.

The school of the future will follow the disciplinary pattern indicated by the black line in the graph in its efforts to teach each child the values and mores of its community.

CHAPTER V

Administration

How Will the School Operate?

The framework of the administrative organization of the school will remain approximately what it is today. The methods and objectives of the administrative program will be modified in the future as will be the function of many of the people and the administrative positions in the school system.

The Board of Education of the future will consist of ten duly elected members of the community. There will be another five members appointed to the Board by the county courts. These members will be chosen from the most responsible members of the community. The entire group of fifteen will be voting members and their terms of office will be six years with overlapping terms for both elected and appointed members.

The function of the Board of Education will be primarily consultive. It will serve as an advisory group to the Superintendent of Schools. More and more will the Board accept the educational principles and procedures of educators and more and more will it spend its time in a consultive capacity representing the community to the schools and *vice versa*. It will retain the community control over the schools through control of the budget and through the authority it has as a group of community representatives to hire the Superintendent of Schools. Its meetings will be open and deliberative, hence any member of the community may appear before it in search of solutions to problems related to education. If there arises a situation where there is school-community friction it will call in specialists from nearby universities and schools of education to gather evidence which relates to the solution of the problem.

The Superintendent of Schools will be in charge of the school at the policy making level. He will have as his advisors, supervisors in each of the following areas: music, art, reading, arithmetic, athletics, science and so on, in addition to other specialized personnel such as psychologists and psychiatrists whom he deems necessary to the proper functioning of the school system. This personnel will report directly to the Superintendent of Schools and will spend its time working with the teachers in the various schools of the district.

The Superintendent will meet weekly with the principals of the schools and will bring to their attention the information and suggestions of his supervising staff. The principals at these meetings will present the problems which arise and solutions will be found cooperatively.

Each year the position of the elementary school principal is given more community status. Each year sees additions in the necessary qualifications for the position of elementary school principal. Each year sees better qualified applicants for elementary school principal vacancies. These trends are in keeping with the increased responsibility which is being given by communities to their elementary school principals through the awareness of the important tasks which he faces.

The elementary school principal of the future will be one of the community's most important and experienced professional workers, for within his organization is laid the foundation of skills, attitudes, and thinking of the future of the community.

Because of the growing complexity of his position, the elementary school principal will be given much specialized assistance. His primary functions will be those of administrative leadership and liaison with the community. He will be responsible for the efficient administration of his school and its proper supervision. He will, in addition, spend much time with parents, both individual parents and parent groups. At such times there will be discussions of various aspects of his school. To him will fall the greatest portion of the social interpretation of the school to the community.

Attendance Services

The day of the truant officer is passing. Delinquency from school is still in great part an administrative and quasi-legal problem. The school of the future will treat attendance services as an educational problem rather than as a legal problem.

Absence from school reflects an attitude toward school. The attendance officer of the future must be psychologically oriented. His prime objective will not be to force children into school but to help them to want to go to school. His function will be one of guidance. His training should be comparable to that of a guidance director trained primarily in the guidance of children who, because of poor adjustment, exhibit deviant attitudes toward school and toward wanting to attend school.

Curriculum Planning

The planning of the learning activities offered by the school will be a comprehensive and cooperative venture. There are certain techniques of curriculum planning and certain curricular areas which educators are best qualified to organize. These areas will be planned and organized by teachers and administrators working at a committee level.

The children of the school will also be involved with curriculum planning. Their interests and wishes will be considered in the overall organization of the curriculum. Parent groups, representative of the community, will have a very active part in planning the curriculum. They will make a basic contribution from the point of view of what the people of the community want for their children and from the point of view of what the children of the community need. Specialists in education from nearby schools of education and from the State Department of Public Instruction will be called in to assist in the planning and organization of the material at a consultive level. All of these groups bring to the curriculum a breadth of information and their cooperation will result in a richer school experience for children and a healthier educational structure for the community.

Finances

The elementary school of the future will need and must have more money. Schools are supported today by local taxation with help from the state. Both the local and state tax bases are rapidly reaching their upper limits, hence the school must look to other sources of income. The various state governments are already contributing a goodly portion of their budgets to education as are local school districts. The schools, however, are in desperate need of more money.

Educators and local school authorities have been opposed to federal aid to education. This aid has been spurned primarily because educators and school authorities feel that federal funds will bring along federal control of schools.

The school of the future will compromise on this problem. It will get the needed financial aid from the federal government. The money will, however, be earmarked for special purposes. As the need for financial assistance becomes more urgent school districts will ask for and receive money for such specialized purposes as the erection of new buildings, building remodeling, buying large pieces of educational equipment, maintaining the health services, maintaining psychological and counselling services, and maintaining the lunch program; all at a subsidized level. Such funds apply at a level other than at the policy making levels which local authorities want to protect and yet will supplement the financial intake of the school district. The trend toward this end has begun with the subsidized school lunch program and will, in light of the success in that area, be both continued and expanded.

Guidance

Problems which defy solution to both teachers and parents will be referred to "guidance counsellors." These counsellors will have training in family relationships and in child adjustment areas in addition to teacher training. Their main effort will be to bring the problem to proper focus and to help the parents and teacher to evaluate the problem validly. In addition, they will refer children and parents to more specialized non-school personnel if the problem defies solution at a home-school level.

Guidance counsellors will be expert teachers who have received extra training in psychology, counselling, and social work. Their responsibilities will include much of the detailed type of counselling service which reverts now to the school principal. They will be specifically trained for such work and will free the principal for other activities.

Health Services

Children will be taught good health habits and attitudes. They A full report of those examinations plus recommendations will be sent home to the parents. A record will be kept of these examinations plus a record of the treatment each child receives for any physical anomaly which may be present. The school nurse will also keep a list of absences because of illness for each child, she will also keep a developmental record for each child and will make periodic checks on each child's general health, how he looks, how he eats, his posture and general expenditure of energy. Visual, auditory and dental examinations will be made periodically on each child by specialists in those areas.

Children will be taught good health habits and attitudes. They will be given a broad informational approach toward fostering their own good health and the good health of others. Their daily activities will be organized with good health and good physical development in mind. Their outdoor activities will be aimed at healthy exercise coupled with the formation of an interest in outdoor activities which will be maintained throughout life.

In-service Teacher Training

In order to augment teacher training and in order to keep the educational practices commensurate with new educational research and thinking, teachers will be given periodic in-service training. The in-service program will be organized and administered from the Superintendent's office. It will include series of combination lecture-conferences by prominent educators, and workshop type activities wherein teachers see good teaching and then discuss the principles involved. In some cases the school board will pay for extension courses taken by teachers at nearby universities. All schools will have a sabbatical leave program for those teachers who want to use it for added training.

In-service training will also be conducted by principals at the individual school level. All teachers will be required to take periodic in-service training.

Inter-group Relations

Good inter-group relations can only be taught in part by the schools. Good or poor inter-group relations find their basis in the community. Only a community which practices good inter-group relations will receive from its school a sound program of inter-group relations. Schools are at present working toward this objective but are making very slow progress. As communities show growth in this area, the work being done by the schools will become more fruitful.

In the ideal world there would be no need for the concept of "tolerance." The most profound change in the field of inter-group relations at the elementary school level will be the elimination of this need. The school of the future will base its concept of inter-group relations at an individual level. It will teach children to evaluate individuals on the basis of what they are as individuals. It will teach them to evaluate individuals objectively and then to accept or reject such individuals as the evidence indicates. It will work toward the elimination of tolerance which implies inequality. Members of minority groups will not be tolerated as members of a group but will be accepted or rejected by all on the basis of what they are as individuals. This process will hold true of all members of the ideal democratic community.

Lunch Program

The school of the future will serve all children a hot mid-day lunch at very little or no expense to the children. This program will be subsidized in great part by the federal government.

Meals will be served in a cafeteria with the school dietitian seeing that each child's choice of foods is well balanced. The choice of foods will be permissive within this framework. In the

event that a child doesn't want to eat some part of his lunch, he
will be allowed to leave that food after first having had a taste of
it.

Much time will be spent in teaching the social aspects of eating
and correct table manners will be discussed and stressed as required social knowledge.

Psychological and Psychiatric Services

Schools are beginning to avail themselves of psychological
services. They have added, in many instances, psychologists to the
staff and are using them in the improvement of education.

The school of the future will use the psychologist primarily to
help to fit the program of the school to the needs of individual
children. This will be concerned primarily with children who exhibit some deviance from the norm in some phase of learning.
The psychologist of the future will also be responsible for evaluating the individual learning taking place relative to each child's
capacity. He will also do so at a group and statistical level.

Psychiatrists are beginning to realize the important obligation
which they have to the elementary school. They are beginning to
enter the activities of the elementary school through the training
of teachers and through dealing with parents of school-age children. There is, however, a residual resistance on the part of all
concerned to the new relationship.

As psychiatry becomes cognizant of its obligations to children
through preventive measures and as it learns to deal with parents
and teachers in a less dogmatic vein, it will begin to assume its
full place in meeting its community obligations.

The school of the future will utilize the great potential of help
which psychiatry can offer as it becomes more aware of the values
of the service and as a real understanding of both the school's and
psychiatry's point of view are achieved.

Both psychiatry and psychology have much to contribute to the
elementary school of the future through their trained practitioners. These practitioners will make a contribution through
dealing in a specialized manner with children and also through
bringing to the attention of teachers as well as parents new findings in their fields. In addition to the above, both these professions

must ally themselves with schools of education in order to present to teachers courses in both areas which will help them to appreciate better the values of psychiatry and psychology, and which will make teachers sensitive to the types of problems which they can overcome in the classroom, if occasion arises.

Relations with the State Department of Public Instruction

The function of the various States' Department of Public Instruction will be that of supplying leadership to education. Schools will look to these agencies for council and guidance. These agencies must supply much of the needed philosophic and research type leadership in education. They will also provide help for those school systems which have educational problems which defy solution at the local level.

Too much of the Department of Public Instruction's present time and resources are spent in setting up minimal standards and programs for the weakest schools of the State.

Relations with Schools of Education

Schools of Education will in the future be very closely allied with the public schools. They will do so because of the mutual benefits which are to be found in such an alliance. Through the alliance, Schools of Education will become more realistic about the problems of teachers, and will incorporate many of the problem situations which teachers face daily in their curricula. They will also become more aware of the role of parents in a healthy school community. They will be called upon more often by the local school authorities for aid in the solution of educational problems and to guide research at the local school level.

Through the five year training program for teachers they will be able to allot more time for visitation and practice teaching in the schools by their students. They will be called upon to help with the in-service training program for teachers in the schools and will provide specialized help and training centers such as psychological clinics, reading clinics and speech clinics to the community. These services will be used by the children who need them for therapy and will serve as training centers for teachers in those specialized areas.

Safety

The physical safety of children in school is becoming increasingly important. The buildings and equipment will be organized and used in the safest ways possible. There will be a standing faculty committee in each school which will constantly evaluate the safety features of the school. The Board of Education will have a committee make a semi-annual evaluation of the safety features of each school. State and local authorities will make periodic evaluations of the schools' readiness to cope effectively with such exigencies as fires, traffic safety and a general community crisis. These safety areas will be incorporated into the curriculum and children will be made aware of hazards to their safety and will be taught how to avoid them.

Sensory Aids to Learning

During the second quarter of this century sensory aids to learning became a fad. Since then most schools have been supplied, many over-supplied, with film projectors, slide projectors, film strip projectors, various models, flannel boards, radios, television sets, and such other materials which were considered sensory aids to learning.

All of these aids to learning made contributions toward the enrichment of the educational process when they were first introduced. As their use became more universal it was found that in many instances their values were much more limited than it had been assumed. This was the result of setting too many and too optimistic objectives for their use and the loss of their novelty to the children through greater use, familiarity, and through their inclusion in many homes and communities as media for entertainment. The aforementioned sensory aids to learning will continue to be used in the future but will be used with discretion for the attainment of the rather specific objectives for which they were designed. Their general use, therefore, will decline excepting for blackboards, bulletin boards, models, collections, and, above all, television. Television is now going through the stage of misuse in education. As it becomes more universally available to teachers it will be misused even more. When the techniques of television have reached maturity and the value of television as an educational aid is evaluated, it too will fall into its proper niche as an excellent adjunct to the educational process with, however, certain limitations as to applicability and as to objectives within the overall framework of the elementary school program.

Special Education

Special education is waning gradually. During the late nineteen twenties and thirties special classes were very much in vogue. Children were homogeneously grouped according to abilities or disabilities. Such grouping made for stereotyped teaching aimed at what was considered a common academic need. It was discovered that other more basic needs were not being met. The school of the future will group children according to social growth. In most other respects the grouping will be hetereogeneous excepting for those who vary a great deal from the norm. The meeting of most specialized and individual needs will take place within the normal classroom situation. In such a climate children will be able to grow in ways which will satisfy their needs and at the same time to live and interact with a cross-section of the population which is representative of the world they will live in when they leave school.

Only those children who are extremely deviant, those who would have a negative effect on the growth of their classmates and those whose physical condition precludes normal classroom life will be set aside in special classes in the school of the future.

Textbooks

At one time textbooks were considered the only content of the curriculum. They were studied chapter by chapter until mastered. Mastery of the texts was the only criterion for success. Such emphasis made education a narrow process. The school of the future will consider texts as tools to learning. They will not constitute the sole source of material but will serve as one of many sources. They will be utilized in the classroom as the need arises. Children in the classroom may have different texts, and may be studying different areas in the same subject field. There will be many sets of texts on the classroom library shelves. Only a very few of these will be bought for universal classroom distribution. The texts will vary in content and level of difficulty. Both these factors will be taken into consideration when books are chosen for specific classroom use.

The Year-round Program

The year-round program instituted by some communities is the beginning of a trend which in time will be universally accepted. The most powerful influences behind this trend are:

1. The more extensive use of expensive buildings and equipment by the community.
2. The provision of healthful activities for children during the summer months. This latter influence is by far the most important and arises from the nature of the way of life in the community. The complexities of modern life and the tendency toward urban living have created a real need for supervised healthful activities during those weeks when school is not in session.
3. The provision of added income to underpaid teachers.

The year-round program of the future will give the school a new community conotation. Many schools are considered today as part time organizations in which children are taught academic subjects. Teachers are considered part-time community workers interested only in the academic phase of childhood development.

Both children and parents will see their teachers and schools in a new light in the all-year program. School will become a place for year-round learning and living in many fields. Teachers will be seen as full-time community workers who are contributing a great deal more to community life than merely the academic education of children.

The administration of the school of the future will be a complex community-based function. Although the administrative system will remain approximately what it is today many specific administrative functions will be modified. This modification will result in better schools at a day to day level and will result in a general educational structure which is contributing to the ultimate fulfillment of our wishes for the future of the children of our community.

CHAPTER VI

Organization

How Will It Be Organized?

The organization of the school into a smoothly running entity will be modified considerably so that it can implement a newer philosophy of education and educational administration.

The following is an outline of the organization of the elementary school of the future.

The elementary school of the future with 350 students will need the following personnel:

1 Principal
14 Classroom teachers
1 Music teacher
1 Crafts teacher
1 Secretary to the Principal
1 Stenographer
1 Stenographer and Telephone operator (combined)
1 School nurse
1 Athletic Director
1 Dietician (plus necessary kitchen help) female
2 Janitors
1 Janitress

The following personnel will be immediately available and will be assigned to the school on a part time basis by the office of the Superintendent of Schools. (Their salaries as a part of the cost of the schools' operating costs herein indicated are partial, the other school units which they service bearing their share of such costs.)

1 Superintendent of Schools
1 Supervisor of Elementary Education (Assistant Superintendent)
1 Full time Psychologist (Assistant Superintendent)
1 School Doctor
1 Athletic Supervisor
1 Music Supervisor
1 Art Supervisor
1 Curriculum Supervisor
1 Director of In-Service Training

The total yearly operating, amortization and maintenance cost of such a school will be between $125,000 and $150,000. Many school systems spend in the neighborhood of $500 per year per student which compares with the maximum figure given above with many fewer services than called for herein.

There will be twenty-five students per classroom. There will be two sections of kindergarten and of grades 1 through 6.

The school will be in session between 180 and 190 school days per year. Summer vacations will tend to be shorter and other holiday vacations will tend to be of longer duration.

There will be about 800,000 to 1,000,000 cubic feet of air space in the building.

Ability Grouping

There will be no such thing as ability grouping by class sections in the school of the future. Classes will be heterogeneous in nature. There will be grouping within the classroom structure by the teacher for instructional purposes. These small groups will be formed on the basis of common need, common interest, and, in some instances, on achievement level. Heterogeneous grouping of the classroom level will give each child an opportunity to grow in an environment which is truly representative of the community and will give to all children experience in living in a natural group wherein there are many deviations of interest, capacity, and achievement. Such a learning climate will provide children with their most basic lessons in realistic democratic interactions and will add depth to their understanding of human relations.

Classification of Students

Promotional practices have varied a great deal. There was a time when children were not promoted until they had mastered a certain percentage of the material presented during the school year. The problem presented by those children who did not have the intelligence to meet the requirements was settled by promoting children "on age" after they were substantially retarded in their progress through the school. This system was unfair to the slow group of students and it did not offer a challenge to the faster group of students.

As a reaction to the weaknesses of this method, because of new knowledge in the area of childhood growth and development, and because of the inception of the progressive education movement, the promotional practice was changed. The reaction was so strong that the change was too drastic. For a number of years we have had a situation wherein there were no criteria for promotion. Promotion under this new system is automatic.

The promotional policy of the school of the future must be based on meeting pupil needs. Because of differences in abilities in children the promotional criteria must be adjusted to the individual. This practice must be tempered by a basic knowledge of community criteria for success.

One of the most basic changes in the promotional philosophy of the elementary school will be the gradual acceptance of the ungraded classroom unit. Children will be classified upon their entrance into the school. The program will be aimed at meeting their specific needs. Their growth will be the most important evaluative criterion relative to success. Their parents will, however, be made aware consistently of growth relative to former status and growth relative to native capacity, as well as to growth relative to the community and over-all group norms for that particular age level.

The first three years of the elementary school will be composed of somewhat ungraded groups. The teacher with whom the children begin the first grade will stay with the same class for three years. Such a plan will enable the teacher to come to know each child very well and would enable her to educate the whole child without arbitrary standards interfering with the growth and movement of the child through the school. At the end of the third grade children will be required to meet a minimal standard of proficiency in academic areas. Those children who exhibit emotional, social, or physical deviation from the group to the extent that they are not realizing full value from the program will be moved back to a group with which they can grow, compete and be happy. Those children who have not achieved the minimum standards at the end of the third grade will be further tested to see whether they should stay in the same group, receive individual help or go on with the group.

The teacher of grades 1 to 3 will meet a new educational program each year and through such experiences will become a master teacher with good insight into growing children. She will test them periodically as will the school psychologist to ascertain their growth over certain periods of time.

Students in grades 4 through 6 will be classified according to grades with a reasonable spread of achievement in each grade. These will be self-contained class groups with a single teacher. If the groups are split according to sex as they will be in most instances in the future, men will teach the boys and women, the girls. These split class groups will have many opportunities for interaction at both the classroom and playground levels.

Class and School Size

The ideal pupil-teacher ratio is somewhere from twenty to thirty pupils per teacher. This ratio depends upon many factors such as class makeup, the teacher, the physical plant and the needs of the community. The ratio will fluctuate from community to community but twenty-five will be near the ideal.

The one-room school will be non-existent in the future. The gradual decline of the one-room school and its eventual demise has been and will continue to be the result of its great expense when compared to the cost of educating children in consolidated schools, the increased opportunities for growth in all areas which are available in the consolidated school, the ever increasing acceptance and ease of consolidation and the tremendous improvement in speed, cost and safety of transportation.

The trend toward consolidation has been so strong that in many instances it has been carried too far. This has been true primarily in urban and semi-urban areas. Many such areas have built elementary schools which are too large. The large schools, although efficient and economically very sound, are not providing as many avenues for individual growths as it had been hoped. These large schools tend to overstimulate or skip-over children. Children tend to lose identity in such schools and are not given as many possibilities for leadership as would be the case in a smaller school. No matter how well planned and organized the buildings and grounds and no matter how well patrolled the immediate traffic dominated streets to the school may be, large schools bring with them a problem of human congestion which is harmful to children. Another great fault of the large school is its unwieldy, large community of parents and required services. A too large community makes good home-school relations at a group level practically impossible.

The elementary school of the future will house from 300 to 400 students, the ideal being 350. The larger urban schools of today will in the future give way to smaller neighborhood schools in which children will grow happily and in which they have a real feeling of participation and belonging. The smaller school of the future will have greater community or neighborhood identification and its function will be better evaluated and better integrated by its community.

Co-education

The battle of co-education versus singular education has been fought for a long time. Neither system is ideal, singular education does not fully prepare for living in a male-female world. Co-education inhibits behavior on the part of both sexes at certain developmental stages. The pressure of the opposite sex tends to police children into less expression and less honest expression than would be typical during certain developmental stages. During those stages at which the presence of the opposite sex inhibits honest expression education will be singular, and during the other developmental stages it will be co-ed. The school of the future will be completely co-educational in grades one, two and three and will become a modified single educational structure during the latter part of the elementary school years and during the early part of the Junior High School years. The secondary school years will be co-educational throughout all of the years of schooling. The children will be given many opportunities for social interaction and boy-girl group activities.

Departmentalization

The elementary school of the future will consist of self-contained classrooms. Children will be taught in all subjects, excepting handicrafts, art, music and, in part, sports, by their classroom teachers. This will also be true in some instances for the foreign language field until all teachers are properly trained in languages.

The self-contained classroom will be the rule for grades 1 through 5. Grade 6 will have partial departmentalization as an orientation procedure for the departmentalized Junior High School program.

Evening Classes

The elementary school of the future will be used for evening classes much more extensively than it is at present. The primary reasons for this trend will be the schools' positive attitude and help toward fostering evening classes and the increasing leisure time which modern technology is making available to parents. Schools will foster evening classes in an effort to improve the knowledge of the citizens of the community and, in so doing, to improve the community. Such community improvement will eventuate in better schools. Schools will also use the evening classes to foster good home-school relations which again tend to make for school improvement. The school will, as a public service, provide educational activities to adults in an effort to enrich their lives through using their ever expanding leisure time in satisfying activity. The satisfying and constructive use of the ever increasing leisure of our populace will be an objective of education at all levels.

Pre-school and Kindergarten

The kindergarten was borrowed from Germany. In 1873, St. Louis opened the first public school kindergarten in America. It has become an accepted part of the public school system and will in the future be a part of every public elementary school. Its prime objective is the socialization of the child within the framework of a school situation. Such socialization helps children to become acquainted with each other and with the restrictions of school life during the year prior to the time when it has been done in the past. Such growth allows them to spend more time with the more academic activities of the first grade and helps them to achieve a real readiness for the activities and work of learning to read.

The most basic change in the kindergarten of the future will be the gradual movement of many of the first grade skills, activities and requirements to the kindergarten level. In the elementary school of the future the kindergarten will not be considered as a place to play and to develop readiness for first grade. It will instead become the real starting point of the elementary school with both social and academic objectives and requirements to be met before entry into the first grade.

There has been a tremendous growth of nursery schools during and since World War II. The growth was in great part the result of the way of life made necessary by the war. Children were sent to nursery schools in most part to free the mothers to work more closely with the national emergency. The growth of the nursery school movement had now reached its peak.

Nursery schools and nursery school enrollment will soon begin to decline. They will be nonexistent in the future because they will not be needed from the point of view of saving mothers' time and because they are not contributing to the all-round development of the child as it had been supposed earlier. Modern research has pointed up the values of spending the third and fourth years of life at home with mother and a few playmates. This evidence indicates that nursery school is valuable only to a very small minority of children. As this evidence becomes universally accepted and as the need for freeing mothers becomes less urgent, the nursery school movement will diminish gradually until only a few will exist for those children for whom it will meet more needs than will life at home.

School Laws

The school legal codes of the various states are going through a very slow evolution toward clarity and good organization. Most of the state legal codes are riddled with archaic requirements which seemed to be logical at the time of legislation. A few states have completely reorganized their school codes. Reorganization of all school legal codes will be accomplished in the future. The reorganized school codes will clarify much of the tangled legal aspect of education and will make educational administration and organization more efficient through the deletion of many of the legislated facets of the elementary school program which interfere with good education in many of the states.

Segregated Schools

Segregated schools will vanish only when America's social problems are resolved. Segregated schools are in most part the result of segregated communities and the cluster of attitudes surrounding such communities. As the American clusters of attitudes become more mature through a successful period of social reorientation which has already begun, and as the fluidity of our populace makes itself fully felt, the very existence of segregated communities will be threatened. The elimination of segregated communities and schools will make for much healthier intercultural and interracial attitudes which in turn will eventuate in the intergration of all groups into the national system of education at a non-segregated level.

School Transportation

The school transportation problem is now at its height. Consolidation, schools which are too large, and general traffic congestion have created this problem. As schools begin to be of the proper size and as the lunch and athletic programs are expanded, the transportation facilities will be used more economically. Fewer units of equipment and personnel will be required to transport a larger number of children. Consolidated schools gradually are becoming surrounded by small communities. The movement toward decentralization of communities will lead to smaller schools, hence to more schools. Parents gradually are becoming more aware of the importance of a child's living near a school and near playmates, hence they are really dealing with this problem when they buy their homes. This trend will be continued and many small communities will rise surrounding schools to which children will be able to walk from their homes. Such schools will have smaller communities from which to draw their student population. Since such communities will be closer to the schools, fewer children will need to be transported to and from school.

*   *   *   *   *   *   *   *

The school services of the future will be organized in the interests of efficiency and the improvement of the learning on the part of the children. School organization will not be traditional in nature but will be fitted to the organizational needs of the community and the school in a rapidly changing world.

CHAPTER VII

Teachers and Parents

How Will We Get Along?

The teacher is one of the most important single factors in education. Teachers must have well-balanced personalities and must be highly interested in children and their welfare. They must be well trained for their positions which are among the most responsible in the community.

The training of the teacher has been a difficult task. There exists a conflict in the emphasis of "content" versus "method" type of learning and teaching.

Until the advent of the science of education, teachers were trained from the content point of view. Their training emphasized the learning of the subjects to be taught. The training stressed learning not only the subjects to be taught, but also those areas of knowledge which would enrich the prospective teacher's concept of the subjects. Such training turned out teachers who were steeped in subject matter, but who knew very little about teaching.

As a reaction to this type of training, the schools of education deleted much of the subject matter courses and substituted courses in methods of teaching. As time went by it became obvious that the reaction had been too strong. Too much time was taken from the content courses and put into courses in method. The teachers knew much more about methods of teaching and about childhood growth and development but they were lacking a basic knowledge of their subject matter which, in many instances, was the same as lacking a real knowledge of the culture.

The teacher training of the future must combine both objectives. It must provide a rich cultural background for each teacher and it must also provide courses in methods of teaching, analysis of childhood growth and development and a good orientation in educational philosophy. The achievement of these goals can occur only by improving the teaching techniques and curricula of the teacher training schools and by making the course of five years duration instead of four. The teachers' colleges gradually are moving in this direction and constantly are re-evaluating their programs in light of future needs.

Another basic change in the training program will be the new method of recruiting prospective teachers by the teachers' colleges. More emphasis will be placed on the intellectual capacities of prospective teachers and upon the personality make-up of the future teacher as it relates to the teaching of children.

These changes will tend to give the elementary school teacher of the future greater status in the community and will tend, through the improvement of education, to justify larger salaries on the part of elementary school teachers. Both of these facts will help in the recruiting of young men to teach in the elementary schools. This has been a long sought goal which will be slowly but consistently met.

The ideal teacher of the future will be willing to cooperate and to share his knowledge and experience with parents and fellow teachers. He or she will be dealt with democratically by supervisors and administrators and his opinion will be sought before policy changes are made. He will be given committee assignments in many areas where he can use his training and experience in improving the schools. His status in the community will increase significantly in the future.

The ideal teacher of the future will maintain the proper balance between the needs of the individuals and of the group. His techniques and his objectives will be fitted to the developmental level of the children. He will provide for many types of learning and through various methods of evaluation will see that definite and adequate learning is taking place.

One of the most important and one of the most basic achievements of the school of the future will be a profound change in the actual running of the classroom by the teacher. This change is already in progress and in some instances has been achieved at a level which can be considered the ideal. As the new child-centered philosophy of education becomes better clarified and as teachers are better able to assimilate the implications of that philosophy, they will gradually take more of the steps which are indicated toward making their classrooms happy places in which each child can grow and learn to the best of his ability.

The following description points up some of the highlights of the classroom atmosphere in the elementary school of the future:

The classroom activities are organized to serve both the needs and interests of the children. The classroom atmosphere is tuned to the development of academic skills and understandings and at the same time toward the development of desirable attitudes. As a result members of the group will feel responsible to the group. The resultant growth will be toward self discipline and responsibility. Allowance will be made for different ways of reacting and for different rates of growing and learning. These allowances will be made by both teacher and pupils.

As children show that they are ready, new learning experiences will be presented to them. They will be given new learning materials and research techniques as they become ready. They will be taught how to study, how to plan, and how to evaluate their own learning.

The children will be taught to accept each other in a free but educational atmosphere. The classroom will be a happy and healthy place where a group is at work. The academic objectives of the group will not be slighted. The group will spend much of its time mastering the techniques of reading, writing, and arithmetic in an atmosphere which is honest and unthreatening.

Special Teachers

Children will in the future spend the entire day with their classroom teacher. This will include lunch periods and recess time. Because of the great strain on the teacher and because this does not provide time for adequate planning, teachers will be relieved for a period each day by teachers of special subjects such as art, choral speaking, dancing, dramatics, handicrafts and music.

These periods will give teachers an opportunity each school day to plan and relax away from the children. It will also give children new environments and people to which they can learn to adjust.

Teachers' Meetings

Teachers' meetings will be held weekly. Classes will be excused early one afternoon per week and teachers will meet with the principal. He will be the moderator and executive planner of the meetings. The meetings will have the following objectives:

1. To improve the daily function of the school organization. This will include group planning of daily schedules. It will concern itself with the organization of those details of school life which interfere with the smoothness of its function. This function of the meetings will enable the school personnel to function as an efficient united whole.

2. To provide in-service training for teachers. This purpose of faculty meetings will be aimed at augmenting the training of the teachers. It will consist of discussions by various faculty committees, the principal, and, on occasion, various supervisory persons from the superintendent's office, educators of note and professors in the nearby colleges. This activity will further the training of teachers by keeping them informed of new evidence in the field of education.

3. Clarify and constantly re-evaluate the philosophy and the program of the school. This will be accomplished through group discussions and conferences which will be tuned toward meeting more of the children's and the communities' needs. Because the program and philosophy of a school should be constantly adjusted to the needs of the community, this activity will be a constant part of the teachers' meetings. Through it the school will clarify its objectives and will unify its methodology. This will in turn help teachers to feel secure through the knowledge gained and expressed and through the realization that the school is being constantly improved.

4. To fit the program to the needs of the children. This will be achieved through group discussion of the individual problems which schools and children present. The method used will be the "case study" method which will allow teachers to seek consultive

information from other teachers and to learn new techniques through the group analysis of case studies.

5. To seek ways of improving instruction and increasing learning. This function will overlap all of the others. It will serve as the coordinating area of the meeting utilizing every technique available to improve the quality of teaching, the function of the school and the learning taking place.

Teachers' Organizations

Teachers' organizations are of the highest caliber. They are constantly trying to improve the quality of education received by children. Such organizations must be fostered and protected by the populace for they represent one of the greatest professional forces toward the improvement of education.

There are two types of teachers' organizations which can in some instances be criticized. These organizations are those which spend their time and money lobbying in the various state capitols for bills which they feel would be of greatest benefit to their members and those which are called "union" and use the threat of strikes and similar techniques for gaining concessions. Both these types of organizations have come into existence in the educational profession because their members felt that they had been treated unfairly and that in solidarity there was strength. The methods used by these organizations have been responsible for the lowering of the professional status of teachers in the eyes of the community. Such organizations will cease to exist as teachers' needs are better met by communities and by state school codes. As they cease to exist teaching will gain more status as a profession and teachers' needs will of consequence be better met. The vicious cycle toward such organizations is changing and in the future the cycle will be one of the opposite nature, toward greater status and rewards for teachers and the elimination of organizations which do not contribute toward the improvement of the educational profession in a universally accepted way.

Teacher Visitation

Each teacher will be given at least two school days per year to visit other schools in action. Such visitations will be reported upon by the teachers at faculty meetings, pointing up differences in procedures and general evaluations of the philosophy which are observed. Each school will in turn be visited by teachers from other schools and other communities.

Schools will be visited periodically by members of the faculties of schools of education and by students in those institutions. These visits will be cooperatively planned and will be mutually beneficial to schools and schools of education.

They will also be visited by agents from the State Department of Public Instruction as a part of that agency's improvement of the schools.

*   *   *   *   *   *   *   *

Prerequisite to good schools are healthy school-community relationships. Parents represent the community in this interaction and teachers the school. Parents' relations with schools will improve as they become more involved with the planning and function of the school and as they become more familiar with the school. The most effective method of helping parents to understand the school and, in so doing, to enlist their cooperation will be through discussion meetings of parents and teachers.

Parent-teacher meetings will be semi-social affairs with the following objectives:

1. To interpret the school to the parents.
2. To interpret the needs of the community to the school.
3. To provide a meeting ground for parents and teachers and parents and parents.
4. To cooperatively work toward improving the schools, and in so doing toward improving the community.

Parent-teacher meetings will in part consist of the school staff describing their individual functions within the school to the community. They will also consist of discussions of the objectives, philosophy, program and methods of the school by both parents and teachers. Another function will be the discussion of the needs of the community by both parents and teachers and the arrival at general and specific needs which the community has and which could be met, at least in part, by the school.

In addition to these educational functions the parent-teacher meetings will be social. They will provide an avenue for interaction at an individual and cross-group level. They will provide a social meeting ground for parents who have children of approximately the same ages and who live near each other. This interaction will add to the natural cohesion of most healthy communities. It will also give parents and teachers an opportunity to meet and interact socially. This interaction will help to make the school community relations progressively more stable and mutually understanding.

The school of the future gradually will become more integrated into the community. It will use the community for study purposes. It will work toward improving the community through the study of community needs and problems. The objectives of the school will be biased in light of the specific needs of the community populace.

More of the curricular content will be related to the community. The community will be the basic workshop of the social studies and it will, by its nature, set up many of the objectives of the school.

Because of the important function of the elementary school in our society, the elementary school has achieved a new status in the eyes of industry, government and other agencies. There is countless material available to schools, most of it free. This material is in the form of books, pamphlets, models and collections. Lay members of the community will be brought into the school to share their experience and training toward the enrichment of the educational program.

Community institutions such as library, hospital, civic playground, and civic entertainment facilities will all be used cooperatively by both community and school.

All of the building and playground facilities of the school will be used by the community after school hours and during school holidays. Such use will be regulated by the school authorities.

School sites in the future will be chosen in light of complete and scientific community surveys. These surveys will tend to locate schools where they will best meet the needs of the community. Such needs will not only include academic needs of children but also will include community activity type of needs.

Communities will, in the future, use their school buildings to a greater degree than at the present time. In addition to the all-year program for the children, the community will use both teachers and buildings in the improvement of the community. Some of the teachers will be teaching parents' groups at night using the school facilities. Civic functions will take place in the school buildings. The school grounds will be utilized by community groups as will their indoor athletic facilities. Week-end community activities and week-end recreational activities will take place in the school of the future. The school of the future will truly become the community center.

The elementary school of the future will be much more involved with the community than is the school of today. Communities will, in the future, be more involved with their schools than they are at present. This community-school involvement will in most part take place at a teacher-parent level. This increase in the school-community interaction will be one of the most fundamental forces toward making the school of the future a very close approximation of the ideal environment for children.

CHAPTER VIII

Tests and Reports

Will They Be Learning Anything?

Evaluating the learning which is taking place, recording those evaluations and passing them on to parents is an area of education which will be modified in great part in the school of the future. The evaluations will become much more inclusive and much more scientific. The reports of those findings from teachers to parents will become more honest and more valid. Parents' reactions to reports will become more understanding and more helpful. In general, all concerned will know more about what learnings are taking place and they will, in light of this knowledge, be better able to improve learning.

"What are the children learning?" has always been important in education. The method of finding out has been restricted, in the past, to pencil and paper tests.

The school of the future will use the following types of evaluation to determine what the children are learning:

1. Pencil and paper tests.
   a. Objective tests.
   b. Subjective tests.
2. Practical situations for application.
3. General modification of attitudes and behavior through knowledge.

Teachers will use all of these methods to evaluate learning. They will give tests which contain completion items, true-false items, matching items, all of a very objective nature. They also will give tests which are general and subjective in nature requiring a paragraph for an answer or the writing of a discussion of the problem.

Teachers will use practical situations for observing the application of materials learned. They will listen to children read in informal situations, see their unassigned written material, watch them use their arithmetic concepts in their projects, and such activities which require application of the material that has been taught.

Teachers also will be sensitive to changes in attitude and behavior through knowledge gained in the classroom. Because education is aimed at the modification of behavior, this will be the most crucial test of the success of the teaching. It will also be carried on in the community by members of the community. The effectiveness of the educational system will reach its height when the behavior of humans in the community is of the quality set up by the schools and homes as the most desirable type that can be achieved under the circumstances.

Children do not have equal talents. Within the same family children's talents show great variation. The scientific measurement of these aptitudes has come to us from the intelligence test movement. Tests of intelligence are all-inclusive, hence their function is somewhat limited for teachers. Recently there have been published tests of intelligence which can be analyzed into various aptitudes. Hence a child not only is given an intelligence score but is also given areas of special aptitudes and weakness. Such an analysis of the ability to learn will help teachers a great deal in the school of the future.

Tests of intelligence will also be given to groups. Children whose scores are markedly deviant from those of the group or children who exhibit weaknesses in crucial areas of learning will be referred to the school psychologist for an individual appraisal and programs which meet their needs will be recommended.

The school of the future will have proficiency standards at the skill level from Grade 3 on. These proficiency standards will be set up in the fields of reading, spelling, writing, arithmetic and general social behavior. Their justification will be in the fact that they are cultural standards which are very necessary for success in America. Obtaining these standards, however, is minimal, hence those children with better than average ability will do much better than the required minimum and those with less than average ability will not do as well. Proficiency standards will serve as norms for achievement, and for prognosticating success in life. Tests of capacity will in each case be used to relate the child's achievement to the norm.

Measurement of personality development is a relatively new facet of education. The scientific measurement of personality development is best done at present through "projective techniques." Children are given ambiguous pictures or situations and are asked to react to them. Their reactions cannot be determined by the situation because it is ambiguous. Their reactions are therefore dictated by their personality which is the basis of the tendency to react to a given situation in a given way. The reactions to these ambiguous situations provide much insight into childhood behavior and will be one of the school of the future's most useful and used techniques in the study of children.

In addition to tests, the following methods will also provide information on the growth of each child.

Checklists of children's emotional growth will be made periodically. How they react to situations and growth of those levels of reaction is of great importance to the child's overall adjustment. Teachers will, through watching children in action and through periodic conferences, register their impressions on the check lists for a developmental record in this area.

Teachers will watch children in their dealings with other children. They will note whether the child's interaction with others is at a level in keeping with his chronological level and with his school placement. Records will be kept of each child's role and status within his group and the development thereof.

Another type of record kept for each child will be cumulative observations by the teacher of each child's behavior. The taking of these records will be systematized through teacher training courses. These records will be taken periodically and will be put into the child's school file.

All of these records will be kept in the school file for each child.

They will be confidential and will be generalized in the reports to the parents. If there is an educational problem they will be brought to the problem as added evidence toward its solution.

In addition to the above-mentioned methods for evaluating academic proficiency, schools of the future will subscribe to multi-community testing services which will furnish tests in the spring and fall of each academic year for all grade levels. These tests will be administered by the teachers and will be corrected and statist-ized at the testing service headquarters. Such services will give a statistical analysis of each group to the school and will analyze the academic proficiency of each child as it relates to norms at a multi-school and multi-community level.

All of this information will be recorded and analyzed. This analysis will be a continuous process. Periodically the parents will be apprised of their child's growth through teachers' reports to parents.

The report of the future will be a three fold process. The most important aspect will be the parent-teacher conference, wherein the child's progress and problems are discussed. In addition to periodic conferences, teachers and schools will send reports to parents. These will consist of objective type marks based on the child's achievement as it relates to group norms. In addition, the report will contain a letter type evaluation of the child's progress. This will consist of several paragraphs written by the teacher. The conferences will, in great part, follow the receipt of the report card and letter from the school. The conferences will be scheduled at a time convenient to both parents and the teachers. These conferences will constitute the most important home-school relationship. Parent-teacher conferences will no doubt go through a stage of being criticized by both parents and teachers until they become a more perfected technique on the part of the teachers and until they become more universally accepted as very valuable on the part of parents.

Generally the following conference technique will be followed by teachers in the future:

The conference will be arranged by the teacher for a conveni-ent time when both parents will be available. Conferences will be held, in great part, at the school. Some few will take place at the child's home. Conferences will be periodic, hence they will not be assumed by the parents to be related to deviant behavior of their child. The objective of the conference will be, therefore, a general discussion of the child's over-all growth and the cooperative formulation of plans for furthering such growth.

Prior to the conference the teacher will review the child's records. She will reappraise all of the child's activities in the classroom relative to the group and relative to the child's specific and general needs. With this information the teacher is prepared to listen and to clarify any problems which might arise in the discussion.

The teacher will greet the parents in a friendly manner in the pleasant surroundings of the conference room which will be free from interruptions. The teacher will not be behind a desk, but will sit in a comfortable chair, as will the parents. The teacher will steer the opening conversation as smoothly as possible to the child's general development. Following the general picture, the parents and teacher will discuss specific aspects of the child's growth. If there is a problem, the teacher will not assume that the parents have come for help, but will assume that the parents have come to work cooperatively in the interests of their child.

If there is a problem which is specialized the teacher will refer it to the proper administrator, being frank about her inadequacy in dealing with such a problem.

All courses of future action on any problems will be the result of cooperative parent-teacher thinking. The teacher will recapitulate the discussion and outline the cooperatively determined course of action. Following the outline of the future course of action the parents will be asked for suggestions as to how the school could better educate their child. After making arrangements for the next conference, the teacher will close the conference on a friendly and optimistic note and will thank the parents for their cooperation and help.

Such a program for evaluating, analyzing and reporting growth will help children, parents and teachers to evaluate the function of the school more validly. It will, through increasing the evaluative evidence and through its proper dissemination, eventuate in an educational structure with a greatly increased effectiveness and a realistically accepted concept of success or failure.

CHAPTER IX

Grounds and Buildings

Where Will It All Take Place?

The school grounds of the future will be spacious with three hundred and fifty square feet of area per child. They will be divided into the following areas:

1. The planted area of shrubs, vines and trees.
2. The turf area for other play.
3. The specialized area and specially surfaced area for all-weather play.
4. Playground equipment and storage area.
5. Age-group areas.

The planted area of shrubs, vines and trees will surround the school building and its purpose will be to enhance the beauty of the building. These plants will be in most part evergreen. This area will be only a small portion of the general playground area.

The turf area of the playground will be the largest area. It will be used for free play and most organized games when weather permits. Different segments of this area will be delineated by tree and shrub lines. There will be large shade trees in the free play area.

The specialized play area will be set aside for certain types of play and will be surfaced for all-weather use. This area will be a relatively small portion of the over-all play space and when its use is made mandatory by the weather its use will be staggered.

The playground equipment will include: two large slides, a

number of swings, two jungle gyms, two large sandboxes, a number of seesaws, and much informal play equipment which can be
used in free dramatic play.

The entire playground area will be enclosed by a heavy wire
fence and will be supervised at all times that children are at play.

School architecture has now reached a point wherein it is meeting the needs of small children. Architects have come to see the
needs of children in a modern classroom and have designed buildings which meet practically all of the needs of children in the
classroom.

The buildings of the future will be simple and functional from
an architectural point of view. Most of them will be single story
structures, excepting in those areas where real estate and building
costs are very high and in those locations where winters are long
and severe. This latter factor greatly increases heating costs and
in some instances these costs may make single story buildings pro-
hibitive from the point of view of the expense of heating.

The basic trend in the design and building of schools has been
the gradual but dramatic shift from permanence to function.
Schools of the past have been built for permanence and long term
amortization in terms of use. The modern school building is
built for function and pleasure of use. It is to be used by children
during the school day, by their parents at night, and by the community during times when the children are not there. This constant and more pleasant use is based on the premise that such use
tends to cut down the period of amortization and will in the
future cut down on the number of schools which are obsolete and
unfunctional, but because of necessity are used by the children.

The construction of the school of the future will be sturdy but
inexpensive. Gone will be the ornate and gone will be solid brick
outer walls or plastered inner walls. Cleaning and maintenance
will be relatively easy and inexpensive. The school of the future
will be constructed from a basic steel and concrete block plan.
Brick work will be veneer only. The concrete block inner walls
will be covered with a light coat of colored cement. Windows will
be metal, as will be all doors and other trim. Roofs will be
permanent and fireproof. Floors will be made of concrete and will
house the pipes for radiant heating. They will be covered with

long-wearing tiles. Ceilings will be finished by having sound-proofing materials fastened directly to the supporting joists.

All-purpose Room

The school will have a large 30 x 30 feet all-purpose room. It will contain a piano and will be put at the disposal of all groups on a request basis for those activities which cannot be comfortably carried out in the classroom. This room will also serve as a room for inter-group get-togethers, such as discussions, sings, planning sessions and assemblies. It will also house small parent meetings and community activities which do not require all of the space provided by the gymnasium-auditorium room. In many ways this room will be one of the most useful and satisfying in the school in terms of use by pupils, teachers and parents.

Art Room

The art room will be much less attractive to the adult eye than it is at present. It will be a functional room with running water and much storage space for smocks and materials. The materials will vary a great deal. They will include paper, paste, crayons, clay, paints and finger paints. The room will have much display space. The general theme of the room will be informality with many artistic materials constantly ready for children to use.

Auditorium and Gymnasium

The auditorium and gymnasium rooms will be the same room at the elementary school level. The high school will have separate rooms for auditorium and gymnasium with permanent fixtures in each as dictated by the needs of the school and the community.

The auditorium and gymnasium will be interchangeable in the elementary school. Along one wall there will be a large stage with curtains. The floor of the room will be tiled. The patterns of the tiles will form outlines for various children's games. Chairs will be movable and there will be adequate storage space for materials along the sides of the room. Basketball baskets will be on rollers and will be stored at the side of the room when not in use.

Bathrooms

Bathrooms will be attractively painted and furnished. The sizes of toilets and urinals will be adjusted to the age of the groups using them. There will be one toilet and basin for every twenty children using the bathroom in any given twenty-minute period of the day.

Cafeteria

The cafeteria will be a large, light, and attractive room separated by a pantry, where the dishes will be stored, from an efficient and hygienic kitchen. It will be tastefully decorated and each plastic topped table will seat about eight children. The walls of the cafeteria will be painted attractively or will be covered with murals. There will be enough room for each child to eat comfortably, to be supervised properly, and not be rushed.

The Classroom

Classrooms will be large square rooms with windows on at least two sides and in the most ideal situation, three sides. The classroom will be bright and airy. One wall will be utilized as blackboard and bulletin board space. Each classroom will contain a library corner and a collection corner to which children can go for information, to share their displays or to chat informally. The arrangement of the furniture will be different for the various grade levels, as will be the placement of learning materials and equipment. The teacher's desk and its placement will be in a secondary position realtive to the general arrangement of the children's desks and the teaching equipment.

Color

The school interior will be painted in non-glossy pastel colors. The classrooms will vary in color. The colors will be chosen relative to ease of vision and beauty. The paint will be washable. The door and window trim will be of a complementary color to the walls, as will be the tiled floors.

Conference Rooms

The conference rooms will be multi-purposed and comfortable. They will contain a table for individual work and will be furnished with comfortable living room type decor and furnishings. There will be one conference room to every four teachers on the staff. These rooms will be used for teacher-pupil conferences, teacher-teacher conferences, parent-teacher conferences and will be used occasionally for individual pupil-teacher work and for small pupil planning and research groups.

Draperies

Most of the classrooms will be equipped with transluscent plastic fire-proof draperies. They will add color and warmth to the classroom yet will not impede the entry of light into the room.

Drinking Fountains

The height of the drinking fountains will vary with their location in the building and the groups using them. There will be one indoor drinking fountain for each forty students. There will be at least two outdoor drinking fountains on the play area.

Furniture

The trend of furniture is toward function and informality. The furniture will be of combination steel and wood construction suited to many uses. It will be light yet sturdy and, above all, movable. Furniture will be adjustable to the size of the children. Furniture will have rounded edges and will be easily stored.

Chairs and tables will be used in grades one, two and three arranged in groups about the room. Desks will be used in grades four and five and will also be arranged in groups. Grade six will arrange its desks in more formal fashion when they are not arranged for group activity.

Furniture will be of such a nature that it can be telescoped when not needed, that is tables which fit under one another and stored on top of one another.

Cots for resting will be of aluminum and canvas construction.

They will be light and sturdy yet easily stacked on top of one another.

Handicraft Room

The elementary school handicraft room will be functional for both boys and girls. It will be stocked with many hand tools and a great variety of materials from which the children can choose to work. This room will have areas or "corners" for working in clay, ceramics, leather, general construction, wood, metal and will have the equipment for finishing work in these areas. It will also be equipped with running water.

Illumination

The illumination of the school of the future will be a combination of natural light and indirect fluorescent lighting. The fluorescent lights will contain "daylight" type tubes and the blue-white type tubes will be eliminated.

Walls will be pastel colored. This will tend to soften the light and will tend to cut down on visual fatigue. Minimally, window space will be at a one-to-four ratio to floor space.

Infirmary

The infirmary will be a centrally located, friendly room. It will be the headquarters of the school nurse. The nurse will inspect age 5, 6 and 7 year old children daily. All other children will be required to see the nurse before returning to class after an absence. There will be two or more cots in the infirmary and there will be ample space for the periodic physical examinations made by the school physician. Here will be kept the files on the children's health history. This room will have a small waiting alcove and will have an adjoining bathroom.

Library

The elementary school library is becoming gradually a place where periodicals and reference books are to be found. Other books are being incorporated gradually into classroom libraries excepting in very large schools.

The school of the future will place great emphasis on the classroom library. Such books will be close at hand and their choice can be guided by the classroom teacher who knows each child's reading level. There will be a rotation system for the books which, in most cases, will be administrated by the librarian. Taking out classroom books for reading will become more informal than the usual library procedure. The school reference works and periodicals will be placed in the school library with the usual reference restrictions placed upon them. The trend will be away from the large formal library to a smaller, less expensive and more functional library. The money saved in building and equipping the large library will be invested in more books for each classroom library. Acquisitions will be made on the basis of readability and interest level suited to that particular class age group.

One portion of the library of the future will be turned over to a compilation of teaching materials and references thereof. Another function of the library will be the circulation of professional books and professional educational journals for the teachers' use.

Music Room

The music room will be large and versatile. It will contain a piano, record player, music stands and a great deal of storage space for records, instruments and music. The walls will be covered by heavy fireproof curtains and the floor will have a heavy fireproof rug to improve the acoustics. There will be adequate space for rhythmic activities and dancing. The room will be large enough to accommodate vocal and instrumental groups at an instructional level. Performances will be given in the all-purpose room or in the auditorium.

Offices

Schools will have at least three definitive offices or office areas. The first office will be that of the receptionist or school secretary. It will house the telephone switchboard and will house all of the office materials, such as duplicating devices, extra typewriters, school stationery and financial materials.

The second office will be that of the principal. In it will be a desk for his secretary, his desk, and filing cabinets containing records for all the students in the school. Adjacent to the principal's office will be a private conference room furnished as a living room, containing a conference table, no desk, and a number of comfortable chairs. This room will be the only room in the school, other than conference rooms, faculty rest rooms, and the music room, which has a rug. All other floors will be covered with tiles.

Rest Facilities for Staff

The staff will be provided with a room which will be both attractive and comfortable. This room will be pleasantly decorated, comfortably furnished and centrally located. It will have two adjoining lavatories and will have closet space for storing personal property of teachers. The faculty room will have an adjoining room which will house an apartment-size kitchen. The size of the room will be related to the number of staff members and will be aimed at providing relaxation for teachers during free periods, before and after school, and will also serve as a meeting room for groups of teachers and of parents and teachers. Although such a room of adequate size will be expensive it will be easily justified by the contribution it will make to consistently good teacher morale.

Soundproofing

Most of the school ceilings will consist of soundproofing composition board fastened to structural joists. This soundproofing tends to cut down fatigue on the part of children and teachers and is slightly less expensive than is the typical ceiling material.

Space Per Child

Each situation will dictate the space per child needs of the grounds and buildings. The following are figures which schools will meet in most part:

OUTDOORS—300 to 400 square feet per child. (About three acres for 350 students.)

INDOORS —30 to 40 square feet of classroom space per child. 300 to 400 cubic feet of classroom air space per child.

Storage Space

Each classroom will have ample closet space. These closets will be used to store supplies and those pieces of furniture and equipment which are used only periodically. The lower grades will have the larger amount of storage space per child because their equipment will be bulkier and there will be more of it. The general ratio will be one cubic foot of storage space to each twenty cubic feet of classroom space.

There will be a main storage room for school supplies where the basic inventory of supplies is kept. This storage room will be supplied during the summer following an annual spring inventory.

There will be storage area on the playground used by the younger children for the storage of wheel toys and other playground equipment which needs overnight storage or protection from weather.

Ventilation and Heating

Radiant heating will be the rule for the new schools. Because of the high cost of mechanical-type blower ventilation, many schools will continue to use direct window ventilation. All windows will be equipped with re-enforced baffles to eliminate drafts. If, because of the nature of the construction of the building, radiators are necessary to the heating system, they will be recessed into the walls and covered.

*   *   *   *   *   *   *

The most basic trend relative to school grounds and buildings will be a change in philosophy. Schools which are symbols of classic beauty, great expense, great permanence, architectural "gems" will all give way to schools dedicated to function. Meeting the needs of the community and its children in the best possible way will be the sole governing factor in planning, building and equipping the elementary school of the future.

CHAPTER X

Forces Behind Trends

Is Change Necessary?

The school trends outlined in the text above are the result of philosophic changes. These changes in educational philosophy are directly related to a number of forces within our culture. Such forces result in the modification of our way of life and of our values. In most instances these forces are operative at a level wherein the cultural milieu is modified. Such modification of our way of life of necessity varies the needs of our populace. Variations in needs must be understood and met by the schools. These forces are inevitable, hence so is the necessity for the evolution of the elementary school.

Here are some of the forces which make modification of education mandatory:

We are coming into an era of history wherein both the liberal and conservative extensions of philosophic thought are being reappraised. During the past few decades conservative thought has been in disrepute in many quarters. The changing social and value structures have given the conservative philosophers a new authority. Their added weight is gradually moving America's philosophic balance toward conservatism.

The world economic imbalances which have resulted in war and famine have become important common knowledge. No longer is one area of the world allowed to live in plenty and others allowed to starve without serious political repercussions. All peoples have minimum economic needs which must be met. The

gradual industrialization of areas of the world which were formerly agricultural in nature has modified the world markets for food
and manufactured goods considerably. This modification tends
to dislocate phases of the economy of all nations. As industrialization increases, the extensive markets of American industry will
in general decrease. The maintenance of a market for the products of industry will be accomplished through the expansion of
domestic consumption.

Until recently there have been no real threats to the concept of
democracy. Although many types of political structures have
arisen and although they have threatened the very foundations of
our democratic institutions, our people as a group have constantly
believed in the supremacy of the democratic way of life. Former
threats to the concept of democracy have been considered in
America as merely transitional. Furthermore, none of them has
arisen from a theoretic structure which was logical or valid. The
present threats to the concept of democracy are based on a
theoretic structure which has been logically contrived. Although
its lack of validity has been demonstrated in many ways and for
a number of years, it represents the greatest threat at both the
philosophic and political levels which democracy has had to face.

The American family has changed. The attitudes toward children are becoming increasingly healthy. Children have achieved
a new status in America. They are constantly becoming a more
important segment of our society. They have been given many
freedoms and much more attention. Although the tendency of
the family unit is toward instability, children are paradoxically
becoming more important within the unit.

The first explosion of an atomic device made the complete re-
evaluation of our value structure mandatory. That explosion
ended and began completely different historical eras. The world's
value structure was shaken by the advent of the atomic age and
its view toward the future must be re-oriented in light of this new
force. The advent of the atomic age brings with it many new
problems and dissipates many of the old.

The overall movement of philosophic thought has been and
will continue to be toward eclecticism. Thinkers have studied what
has come before and have moved forward from that point. In

their research into these ideas, they have found many to be of value. They have also achieved a perspective through this research which is broadening their philosophic bases for thought. This tendency helps them to be better able to accept those truths which have come before them.

Cultural interaction is increasing. Intercultural education is becoming more universal. As this occurs, intercultural attitudes become greatly modified. Such modification of attitudes in turn tends to make for changes in behavior. These changes in interaction bring with them many new vistas for great cultural growth and many new and highly complex social problems.

The constantly increasing evidence in the social sciences tends to simplify the adjustment which humans must make to the environment. As the evidence increases, cultural trial and error will decrease. Individual trial and error in the adjustment area will also tend to decrease. Adjusting to the world of the future should be a more simple process as this new information is assimilated and taught by the schools.

America is growing. The elementary school population far outstrips the available space and will continue to do so for a number of years. The increased birth rate will eventuate in a greatly increased general population, school population, work force, and consumers group. The gradually increasing longevity of our population poses problems of meeting the needs of an older group which are not being met today.

The psychological reaction to a half century of near disaster and almost constant war has been of immeasurable intensity. The world's political instability has tended to make whatever class structure which existed in America very elastic. It has modified our concept of the family and the community. Our population changes residence constantly, many individuals making two or three geographic home changes in a lifetime.

Religion has assumed an increasing importance in the lives of Americans since the war. This revival has had a double effect. The first effect is the tendency on the part of those participating in the revival to seek absolute truths. This movement has counteracted the pragmatic thinking in some areas of our daily lives. In those areas values are becoming solidified and no longer vulnerable because they fall down under certain experimental or practical situations. The second effect is the increase of the schism between the religious philosophies and the secular philosophies. Values tend therefore to drift toward one or the other. The middle ground is gradually diminishing.

This century has seen a phenomenal advance in technology. Every area of living has been changed during the last half century because of a rapidly advancing technology. These advances have to a degree conquered both time and space. We move about with great ease and with relatively small expense. We need to spend less time in accomplishing our daily household tasks or in meeting daily production needs.

These forces toward cultural change and their concomitant expression in the modification of the elementary school are inevitable. The elementary school of the future must constantly re-evaluate its position within this volatile cultural framework and must constantly re-orient its practices in light of the changing needs of the community. The elementary school of the future must be a dynamic institution which will be the expression of the needs of the community with each passing year and must remain on the frontier of the culture in its never-ending evolution toward the ideal. Because of its dynamic nature, the function and the purpose of the elementary school can be validly evaluated only in light of the degree to which it meets community needs at any given moment and its relative position in the evolutionary process toward the future and toward the ideal.